WALKING TALL

By the same author
THE SPECIAL YEARS

WALKING TALL

Val Doonican

Elm Tree Books · London

First published in Great Britain 1986
by Hamish Hamilton Ltd/Elm Tree Books Ltd
27 Wrights Lane London W8 5TZ

British Library Cataloguing in Publication Data

Doonican, Val
    Walking tall.
    1. Doonican, Val   2. Singers—Biography
    I. Title
    784.5'0092'4   ML420.D69

    ISBN 0-241-11924-3

Typeset by Redwood Burn Ltd
Printed in Great Britain
by Redwood Burn Ltd, Trowbridge

I can't think of a better dedication
than the one I used in my first book –

To both my families, old and new,
and to the entire cast of this book

—— Acknowledgments ——

The author and publishers would like to thank the Radio Times and Don Smith for their help in supplying photographs for this book: p.6 (with Dickie Henderson); p.7 (both pictures); p.8; p.9; p.10 (with Bing Crosby); p.12 (both pictures); p.13 (in autogyro); p.14 (with Ray Charles and with John Denver); p.15 (all pictures); p.16 (Fiona and Paul Daniels).

Other photographs courtesy of Syndication International (p.2 both pictures of the family, p.11 the family); Peter Emmett (p.3, the cast at Blackpool); H.A. Hallas (p.3, OBE celebration); Ron Howard (p.4, both pictures); Blackpool Gazette and Herald (p.10, playing golf); Gus York (p.16 with Lynn; and the Doonicans now).

Pen drawing of the entrance to Beaconsfield Golf Club

—— Chapter One ——

Yes, I can truthfully say that 'it took me seventeen years to become an overnight success'. My first innocent steps into the unpredictable world of the wandering minstrel were taken 'way back in 1947. Oh! I'd been smitten by the joys of making music, however indifferently, long before that, but fate, in the form of unemployment and little hope of anything else, made my decision to pack my bags and take to the road inevitable. The seventeen years which were to follow formed a kind of endless apprenticeship which I'm happy to describe, in retrospect, as having been filled with enjoyment, hope and invaluable experience. I've already written at some length about those *Special Years* which, even though I didn't know it at the time, were preparing me for a most unexpected bonus ahead.

My own radio series in the early sixties followed by a 'fairytale' style sequence of events led, in time, to a fateful appearance on the television show *Sunday*

1

Night at the London Palladium. The impact of that first eight minute spot was such that it inspired me to coin the phrase quoted in the first line of this chapter. The occasion was, in fact, the climax of a period of some two or three years when I felt I was what I can only describe as 'almost successful'.

The radio show I mentioned was transmitted just one morning each week. I had an orchestra in the studio which under its conductor supplied some of my vocal backings and several of their own musical contributions. I wrote and introduced the show, read listeners' letters and sang requests either with the musicians or to my own accompaniment. For all of that I was paid eight guineas per show. The financial lifesaver was my being allowed to orchestrate my own backings for the band. That brought me another thirty pounds or so each programme.

When I say that the weekly shows were very popular, I suppose what I mean is that they were the most popular thing I'd ever done up till then. One thing I was to learn the hard way is that popularity affects the public a bit like dry rot affects a house . . . *it takes a long, long time before you see any evidence of its being there.* However, I was grateful for small mercies and by the early sixties I could see at least a faint glimmer of that shining light of good fortune.

Now, I was being booked for the odd week's cabaret around the country, coupled with a smattering of one night engagements nearer home, so I thought it was time to treat myself to such niceties as a more expensive stage suit and a better car. My previous models had been an Austin A40 and a Triumph Herald. Now parked outside my door was a gleaming, if second-hand, Mark X Jaguar. I felt a certain glow of pride when I loaded the boot with the tools of my trade, guitar, amplifier, collapsible stool (which I still use today), my personal baggage, and of course, the obligatory plastic suit-cover containing my stage-wear. A fond farewell to Lynn and I'd be off through the gates of our semi-detatched en route to that week's destination. At least I *looked* more successful.

The entertainment industry, however, never fails to serve up a varied sequence of events guaranteed to keep all its staff in a permanent state of insecurity. Just when you think that maybe you've at last 'got it cracked', as they say, it does a Barbara Woodhouse and gives your choke chain a smart pull, just to remind you who is doing the driving.

My racing green Jag sped along the M1 Motorway heading for Yorkshire where, for one week, I was to be the 'star' of one particular club's entertainment.

'VAL DOONICAN AND FULL SUPPORTING CAST', I thought as I relished my new-found status. I wondered who he, she or they would be. A few hours later, pulling up outside a somewhat shabby establishment, I found my answer. A handwritten poster on the wall by the entrance boasted ALL THIS WEEK ... VAN DOONIGAN OF BBC FAME ... PLUS ... THE LOVELY TANYA. Even in those early days I was quite used to people spelling my name with a G, instead of a C, but the VAN was something new. It made me sound like a Dutch clog dancer. All notions of stardom were to fade as that day went on, and I could feel the choke chain tighten. The organist who was to accompany me played badly and cared even less, my dressing room was minute and quite filthy, and my digs were not much better.

'Who is the lovely Tanya?' I asked myself as the landlady cleared the table after a surprisingly tasty dinner. I popped upstairs and had a shave and brush-up before going to face my public.

All was to be revealed, in more ways than one, when I got to the club a little later. The minute dressing room I mentioned also happened to be the only one there, and I was to share its luxury with the lovely Tanya. She was a stripper.

'Hallo, chuck,' she greeted me as I entered. There she sat, unadorned and unabashed, gazing at her reflection in the dust-covered mirror as she busied herself decorating the tools of her trade with a pretty arrangement of sequins.

'Oh hello,' I answered, not bothering to shake hands and turning to hang my suit on the nearest nail.

'Noisy bloody lot out there,' she warned. 'Mind you, it'll bother you much more than it will me.' She looked a bit oriental, in spite of sounding like Hilda Ogden from *Coronation Street*. As she spoke she rose, stubbed out her cigarette and slipped on a multicoloured housecoat. In no time she was introduced to the waiting males and proceeded to do whatever she did, apart from the obvious – I saw nothing from our little room. I decided to change into my mohair suit.

Bless her, she was certainly right about the audience: it was very noisy and bothered me more than it did her. I must say, I developed quite an affection for Tanya as the week went by. She told me she was married and had come out of retirement for a while because they needed some extra money. She was a real 'honest to God' kind of lady and turned out to be the only good thing about that week.

When Saturday night came around it was a bit like Armistice Day or end of term, and I was happy to get away.

'Where are you next week, chuck?' Tanya asked as I packed my things away.

'I'm doing a double,' I told her. 'Chesterfield and Greasbrough.'

'Oh you lucky thing,' she mumbled, pulling on her fur boots for the journey home. 'I've got nothing for weeks ... Ah well, me old man will be outside ...

Tarra chuck, have a safe trip...' And she was gone, never to be seen again by yours truly.

The following week turned out much better, even though it meant doing two shows each night with a car journey in between. On Monday, I rehearsed at both rooms, then went back to my digs. My nightly routine would be to do Chesterfield first, then dash over to Greasbrough, which is just outside Rotherham: a distance of about thirty miles.

My ego was fully charged by midweek, the act having gone down quite well at both venues. Thursday night was my best so far at Chesterfield. Elated, I packed my gear into the boot of my car and took the short cut I'd now memorised along the back road towards Rotherham. It was raining as I found a parking space behind the Greasbrough club. I left the car, put my back against the stage door (kept locked from the inside), and gave a couple of hefty knocks with my heel. A dozen or so kicks later I was still there in the drizzling rain. I wondered how long the door would survive this kind of treatment, night after night, week in, week out. Panic began to set in, as I heard the music heralding the final few minutes of the preceding act, a black lady jazz-singer from America. 'I'd better try the front entrance,' I thought and went dashing through the rain to the other side of the building.

The music, the applause and indeed the temperature trebled in volume as I entered the sticky atmosphere of the reception area of the club. The only evidence of my week's engagement I could find there was a blackboard, my name written boldly across it in chalk.

A plump man with a red friendly face greeted me.

'Evnin' young man...' he almost shouted, then, showing no sign of recognition, went on: 'Are you a member?'

5

'No, I'm in the show for the week,' I panted, 'and the stage door is locked.'

'It always is, sir,' he said, laughing and obviously not believing a word I was saying. 'You'll have to knock, and they'll let you in.'

'But I have knocked and nobody can hear me . . .' Frustration was creeping into my voice by now. 'I'm due on stage in a few minutes, please let me go through the club.'

He was like a brick wall, but still smiling and friendly. 'Sorry, sir, nobody goes through this way but members and ticket holders.'

I thought it was time to play my trump card. 'Look! I pointed hard to the blackboard. 'That's me, I'm Val Doonican.'

Suddenly the little man stopped smiling. He stared straight into my face, his right index finger pointing up my nose, and his attitude changed to that of a man who had a little power and was about to use it.

'Now listen, son,' he began with a kind of menace in his voice, 'it's like I said, nobody gets past here except members and their guests . . . and even if you are Val Whateveritis it makes no never mind to me.' He waited as if daring me to argue with him. I had no intention of doing so, having accepted by now that it was a lost cause. His finger still pointing menacingly into my face, he delivered his 'checkmate'. 'I wouldn't give a bugger if you were Johnny "Goon" Tweed.' He sprayed the words at me. 'You'll not pass here.' He turned and walked away.

By this time I was boiling with indignation and frustration. Storming through the doors I almost welcomed the cooling drizzle on my face as I made my way along the sides of the club. In my rage I'd almost forgotten about the show, when the friendly voice of the stage manager brought me back to reality. 'Don't worry, mate, you've plenty of time, and we brought all your gear in from the car.' He was waiting by the back door holding a golf umbrella aloft as he greeted me. Minutes later it was as though nothing had happened. I stood by the side of the stage all ready to go, and sipped a mug of warm tea. My tragic story was related to the cast as we chatted away the final minutes of the interval. Their sympathetic grunts suddenly changed to hysterical laughter when in all innocence I asked, 'By the way, who's Johnny "Goon" Tweed?' In my ignorance of the club circuit I was unaware that he was one of the most successful attractions at that time. *'Sit,'* I thought to myself in anticipation of the tug on my collar.

I'd like to come back briefly to this question of popularity, or fame, or any other name you'd like to call it. It's something I feel we should keep more firmly under control, and so avoid being too bruised by that choke chain.

There are so many steps in that ladder of success, all of them to be relished and appreciated, but very few people, if any, ever get to the very top rung.

In 1975 I was playing golf with the great Bing Crosby, and you won't find many people on a higher level than he managed to reach. A youngster in the crowd asked his dad if it would be permissible to ask for my autograph. At the appropriate moment he approached and requested a message to Alistair. I obliged, and as I was about to leave I overheard him whisper to his father, 'Is that man with Val Doonican a star as well?' To him, at least at that moment, I was better known than Bing.

We all know that a local personality in Glasgow or Los Angeles can be completely unknown in London or New York. A top flight entertainer from Britain can go to Spain and be a complete nonentity until he bumps into somebody on holiday from Wigan.

The point I'm trying to make is that we are not as important to the outside world as we are sometimes led to believe, so it's best never to assume that the next engagement will be easy, or that at last 'you've arrived'. In my experience at least I have found that people have much more important things to worry about, and we are simply a little light relief. All of us 'in the media' can get a bit too close to its activities at times. The result being that it becomes self-indulgent, over-commercialised and sadly, on occasions, dishonest.

My radio programme continued to flourish, however, and I spent all my available time collecting, adapting, composing and arranging songs to swell my ever-improving repertoire. My publisher Alan Paramor was constantly on the look-out for suitable material for me and took both a personal and professional interest in all my activities. Alan rang me at home one evening:

'I think I've got a great song for you,' he told me. 'There's a young American lad visiting London at the moment, and trying to make some inroads as a composer. He's brought in quite a few numbers, one of which is a Mexican-type song. I think you could do it with the guitar. It's called *Carlos Domingues*.'

I was due at the BBC Maida Vale studies next morning to do my radio show.

'Tell you what, Alan,' I said, 'I'll come over after the show and have a coffee . . . you can let me see it.' We agreed on midday.

When I arrived at the office, Alan was all set to sit at the piano and play the song through. By some amazing turn of fate, he had only reached the end of the introduction when there was a tapping at the office door. Alan stopped. 'Come in,' he shouted. His secretary popped her head around the door.

'Sorry to bother you,' she whispered, 'there's a

gentleman to see you.' Alan stood up as she ushered in a dark-haired young man wearing a smart 'city' type suit.

'Well, talk about the devil,' Alan laughed, offering his hand to the newcomer ... 'We were just playing your song. This is Val Doonican ... Val, this is Paul Kane.'

We all three sat down and had coffee. I loved the song, by the way, and did it many times on the radio. I was to record it some time later, when I made my first album. Now, the only reason I have told you this story is that the young man in question was to become one of the great names in the world of popular music. His 'other name' was Paul Simon. His music is constantly played in our home, and I often wonder with the huge success he's had, and the hundreds of songs he's written since, if he'd even remember having written *Carlos Domingues*.

I spent a good deal of time at home, which was marvellous from a family point of view. We were expecting our first baby and naturally I wanted to be with Lynn as much as possible. My radio work involved hours of just sitting writing music. We turned our spare room into a temporary music studio: I managed to find a second-hand mini piano and attached a draughtsman-style worktop to its front, then, perched on a stool, I'd get on with the job. All day long I'd work on my arrangements for the orchestra, and having completed the scores, change my role to that of copyist and proceed, with pen and ink, to write the separate parts for the members of the orchestra. It really was a chore at times, but once again, it turned out to be of great value in the years that followed.

London wasn't the easiest place for me to find any other form of work, however. Cabaret and stage work were areas where at least for the moment 'I wasn't very well in'. One of the rare dates to come my way in 1963 was a week at the Astor Club in Berkeley Square. My salary was to be £90. A fortune, you might think. I thought it a bit too good to be true until I received the full details. I was to do six shows at the Astor, usually at about one o'clock in the morning. I would also do three extra performances at the Columbia Club in Bayswater Road (a house for the exclusive use of officers of the American forces) and a further three spots at the Douglas House, situated a block further along (a similar establishment for the non-commissioned officers). I agreed to do the twelve shows for the above-mentioned fee. At least I knew I'd have that income coupled with the money from my radio show and arranging: all in all a great week.

What I didn't know, however, was that fate was about to intervene in the form of one of the great tragic events of that decade. Just as my marathon week got underway, the media announced the shattering news of John F. Kennedy's assassination in Dallas, Texas. All entertainment for the American forces was immediately cancelled, and I was informed with much regret that my salary was to be adjusted 'pro rata', as it's described.

I'd like to digress for a moment and relate one of my favourite show business stories, which the previous incident brings to mind.

In the old days of the Music Hall a variety show is booked to appear at a certain small provincial theatre. Monday morning rehearsal finds one of the 'turns' down with flu and with no hope of appearing that week. The company manager desperately rings the head office in London and asks for assistance in the form of a replacement. After much to-ing and fro-ing nothing has been achieved and panic begins to take over. The theatre manager, who is a local chap, thinks he might have at least a 'beggars can't be choosers' kind of suggestion.

'There's an old guy who lives here in town who used to tour the Halls years ago,' he tells the relieved company manager. 'He was a magician of the old school, he's in his seventies now, but I'm told he's helped out several times over the years.'

'Really? How did he go?' queries the company manager. 'I mean, can he still do an act?'

'I honestly can't say,' answers the theatre manager. 'It was before my time, but I do know he's stepped in before on a few occasions.'

The old pro is contacted, his dress suit dusted and pressed and his ancient props retrieved from the attic. He is given a six minute spot in the first half of the bill.

Well, his appearance is a disaster: he forgets his words, he drops his props, and messes up his illusions. After the interval a shattered company manager comes into his dressing room, only to find him quietly packing his little stage basket. The manager forces a smile as the old man turns to greet him.

'Wonderful spot, thank you very much,' the visitor says, having prepared his script carefully. The old man nods his thanks, a knowing look in his eye.

'We're very grateful to you,' the manager continues, 'but believe it or not the show is now running a bit long ... so, I feel awful about it, but we don't really need your spot.'

The old man continues his packing. 'That's perfectly all right, sir,' he says softly. 'It's no trouble at all.'

The manager stands there rubbing his hands with embarrassment. 'That's very understanding of you,' he says, relief written all over his face. 'Ah, I don't quite know what to do about money.' He waits.

'Well,' says the old fellow, 'there's twelve shows for the week, and in the past I've always been paid *a twelfth*.'

I managed to get through my six contracted performances at the Astor Club, however, in spite of all the
problems that particular room presented. It was
almost impossible to achieve any lasting attention
through the barrage of conversation, coupled with
the sounds of food and drinks being served and con-
sumed. I knew the room of old, of course, since my
days with the Four Ramblers, an Irish vocal group
with which I worked from 1952 until 1959. We played
the club several times during that period and even
though we had each other as moral support it was invariably a daunting experience. I was out there on my
own now and felt the full brunt of opposition. One
good thing about the Astor, however, was that many
important people went there for late night susten-
ance. Agents, managers, producers, not to mention
well-established entertainers from round the world
would sit and watch your efforts at point blank range.
I recall doing our act one night in the fifties while the
great Danny Kaye sat at ringside. I might add that he
was very attentive and made us feel good.

There was another memorable occasion when the
American comedian Alan King was present, accompanied by a visiting group of black singers/
musicians, the Trenniers. They were appearing at the
London Palladium for a week, and had called in at the
Astor after their show. A fascinating incident
occurred.

First, I should give you an idea of what the nightly
ritual was from the floorshow point of view. After an
evening of dancing and dining, things usually got
underway with a dance routine featuring the Astor
Girls. This would be followed by the first part of the
entertainment, such as a stand-up comedian. There
would be a little pause, then a second appearance by
the girls. By now the room was normally packed with

Sea grape. Like most of the illustrations in the book, this was done on holiday in Antigua, West Indies

latecomers, the time being around one o'clock in the morning. The top of the bill then filled the final forty minutes or so of the evening's entertainment, to the accompaniment of the resident band led by Johnny Silver. There were, in fact, two bands which alternated throughout the night, the second one featuring Latin American-style music.

As the Four Ramblers took their final bows, I remember that the club's resident host would leap on to the stage and take the microphone.

'Thank you, thank you,' he would shout enthusiastically. 'Come on, ladies and gentlemen, let's hear it for the Four Ramblers.' His encouragement would coax every last bit of appreciation out of a sometimes indifferent crowd. 'Weren't they fantastic, ladies and gentlemen? The Four Ramblers, and they will be appearing every night this week.' He would then go on to announce the coming attractions for the next month or so. Before there was time for the room to lapse back into a blur of conversation, he'd continue . . .

'But the night is still young here at the Astor Club, so we want you to let your hair down and *enjoy yourselves*. Yes, *enjoy yourselves* . . . 'cause *it's later than you think* . . .' This was the cue for Johnny Silver and the boys to play the musical pick-up for what I can only describe as the longest medley of old chestnuts imaginable: *Enjoy yourself, it's later than you think* . . .; *Toot toot, Tootsie, goodbye* . . .; *I'm Alabamy bound* . . .; *Nothin' could be finer than to be in Carolina* . . .; *The stars at night, are big and bright* . . .; *Maammy . . . Maammy, the sun shines east* . . .

And so it went for some fifteen minutes, or at least so it seemed, with everybody dancing, singing and, like the man said, *enjoying themselves*. It really worked, too, and remained a part of the room's 'tradition' for as long as it existed.

Then followed another interlude when everybody who was anybody among the patrons would be introduced in a blaze of spotlights and applause. The celebrities in question would stand up and bow their acknowledgment, wave to one and all, then sit down.

As is the case in many night spots, if there was the slightest inkling that some extra encouragement might possibly inveigle the said party to come to the stage and say hello, or say a few words, or even sing a few bars of a song, then no effort would be spared. Many well-known entertainers had done so over the years and set a kind of precedent, so who could blame a management for trying?

On the night in question, the old routine went as usual. We did our act, took our applause and retired to our room. The medley of songs came and went and the introductions began. Some 'lesser names' were announced to begin with and then came the 'biggies'.

'Ladies and gentlemen, making a welcome visit to the London Palladium, a very talented group of musicians and singers from the United States ... will you meet and greet the fabulous Trenniers.' There was wild applause and cheers as the lads rose for a few brief seconds to accept their welcome to the club.

'And seated right at the same table, we're proud and pleased to introduce one of the world's great comedy talents ... Ladies and gentlemen ... the fantastic, the fabulous MISTER ALAN KING.' Alan King's reception really was something, his popularity in London at that time being one of the talking points among entertainers. He'd appeared for a short season with the great Judy Garland not so long before and made the most amazing impact with the public and press alike.

The applause went on and on while Alan took bow after bow, waving an open hand in appreciation, the customary huge cigar perched between the first and second fingers. He sat down for what he hoped was the last time, turning his attention once again to his guests. The applause continued, reinforced with shouts of 'More' and 'We want Alan.' Mr King tried to ignore it, hoping it would go away, but it didn't. Mein host took what he felt to be the most logical step.

'Would you like to just step up here, Alan, and say a quick "Hello" to the folks?' Alan King declined, waving once again, this time adding a shake of the head as if to say 'Thanks, but no thanks.' The clapping and cheering at last began to fade, when from one of the tables a somewhat disapproving voice shouted,

'Oh come on, mate, stop playing hard to get . . . tell us a few jokes . . . it won't cost you anything.'

There was a smattering of self-conscious laughter mixed with a sort of shocked silence, and all eyes were on Mr King. He positively glared at his critic, then slowly but deliberately rose from the table and approached the cabaret floor. Once again the room rang with applause while the atmosphere changed to that of an audience watching a gladiator entering the arena. He bowed to the crowd, shook hands with the host and calmly took the microphone. Now, I can't claim to be able to quote word for word what went on in the next ten minutes or so, even though I can look back on it as a memorable occasion in my career. The script should read something like this:

(It will help, of course, if you are familiar with Alan King's work and style, that kind of Marlon Brando-ish way of talking, his whole script seeming to consist of complaining about everything. It will also help to know that his assailant in the audience was a short, bald-headed, middle-aged but prosperous-looking man, who sat at a table for two, accompanied by a very young, very busty hostess. He also looked

16

Jewish, and since Alan King's humour can be very much in that idiom at times we were set for a good encounter.)

ALAN: Good evening, ladies and gentlemen, and thank you very much. I'd like to say that it's good to be here, but I can't, because it's not. It's good to be in London. I enjoy London.

I'm over here doing some television shows . . . I've been in the studio all day, rehearsing . . . I got through at about eight o'clock . . . went back to my hotel and had a shower. I then picked up my friends the Trenniers at the Palladium and we thought we'd go out and have a quiet meal . . . Then some joker told us to come here . . . (*pause*). I've just had the worst meal I have ever eaten . . . some clown of a waiter has spilled the most expensive whisky in England all down my pants . . . and now, just to round things off . . . you've got me working again.

INTERRUPTION: Oh come on, you'll make me cry in a minute . . . tell us a few jokes.

Alan paused, puffing on his cigar, then thoughtfully gazing at the burning end the way cigar smokers do.

'Do you think we could have a little light on this guy over here for a moment?' he said, slowly approaching his victim. The spotlight operator duly obliged. The two men were face to face for the first time. Alan looked him over, then looked at the young companion. With a wicked smile on his face he moved his gaze around the room, as if inviting everybody to take a look. The crowd were loving it.

'Good evening, sir,' he began. 'Would you mind telling me your name?' The man, looking very annoyed, refused to be drawn.

ALAN: Come on now, what's your name? You're not going to tell me, are you? OK, tell you what, I'll have a guess. (*Steps back, places his fingers on his pursed lips in a thoughtful pose and smiles.*) Let's call you Louis for now, all right? Now, tell us, Louis, what do you do for a living?

(*Man stares in silence.*)

ALAN: You're not going to tell me that either, so I'll have to guess again? (*Stands back as before and sizes up his new partner.*) I'd say, Louis, ah, you make ladies' skirts in a little back street somewhere in London, am I right?'

(*Man looks more determined than ever to take no part in the encounter, but the expression on his face indicates that he could happily strangle Mr King. At this point Alan King leans on the edge of the table and faces the audience.*)

ALAN (*waving his cigar like a conductor's baton*): I'd like to give you a hypothetical situation, ladies and gentlemen. I want you to imagine that Louis here has had a really tough day in his little factory in that back street in London. At nine o'clock in the evening he locks up his front door and gets into his car to go home, when up comes Alan King. 'Just a minute, Louis,' I say. 'Before you go home I'd like you to give me fifty ladies' skirts.' Now, I wouldn't be a bit surprised if Louis told me where to go. He'd have every right to say, 'Why the hell didn't you come during the day when I was open for business?' (*Pauses and turns to the man.*) Isn't that what you'd say, Louis? (*By now, nobody expects the man to answer, so their eyes go back to Mr King. He then delivers his crushing tag line.*) But you haven't heard the worst yet, Louis, not only do I want the fifty ladies' skirts after working hours, *but I want them for nothing*!

The room erupted to what was the best part of the evening's entertainment as Alan prepared to retire to

18

his table. Then he turned once again to the man and delivered yet another stinging remark.

'I do hope I haven't embarrassed you too much, Louis,' he said apologetically, 'especially in front of your daughter.'

He returned to the cabaret floor, thanked the patrons, and then to everybody's surprise, introduced the Trenniers once again. The boys rose as one and joined him at the microphone. He turned to the pianist and asked for a chord in E flat. Together they closed the proceedings with a marvellous version of the old classic *Up a Lazy River*.

Some years later I watched him do his full cabaret act at Caesar's Palace in Las Vegas. He was quite superb that evening, but for me the name Alan King will always mean that little interlude at the Astor Club all those years ago.

One of the people who popped in to see my efforts at the Astor that week in 1963 was a well-established agent and manager, Eve Taylor. In fact, I didn't know she was there, but a message came through to my room asking if we could have a chat. We met at her office in Regent Street the following week and agreed that we'd sign a working contract for a six month trial period. (Up till then I hadn't had a manager.) We decided that if all went well we'd continue our relationship, and if not, then there would be no point in forcing the issue. Eve was to be my business manager for nearly twenty years. She said she would fix me some badly needed dates in London and arrange for some people to come along and watch me work.

The first booking to come along was a week at Quaglino's Restaurant in Duke Street. I was to do two shows each evening, the first one in the upstairs dining room, and one much later in the basement nightspot known as the Allegro Room.

There were never many people there for the earlier show. This had little or nothing to do with me, of course, since at the time I wasn't a name and couldn't be expected to attract customers in to dinner at a certain time. I worked to about fifteen people on some evenings.

On one of those very quiet nights I was doing my act sitting on a stool, all the tables in front of me being empty except for one solitary lady eating alone. She was very elegantly dressed in a neat blue and white suit. She looked, then ate, then sipped her wine, then looked again, then smiled, then ate again. I sat there and sang, and chatted, and smiled. I think she probably felt a bit sorry for me actually, 'cause she clapped much more than I deserved.

As I sang a gentle little song with the guitar while the resident quartet on the bandstand took a breather, she put down her knife and fork, giving me her full attention. Then I noticed she was pointing in my direction, her eyebrows raised fractionally as though she was surprised. I just sang on. She did it again as if warning me of somebody sneaking up behind me. I gave a sideways glance over my shoulder, but was none the wiser. She did it again, this time with a bit more feeling. Slowly I felt a warm glow of sweat forming on my forehead ... 'Your flies are undone' was written crystal clear in the gesture which she repeated once again. It's amazing, but even though I calmly went on with the song, 'she knew that I knew'. She put her hands down and her face broke into a knowing smile. I sang the final verse of the song on autopilot while I madly worked out my plan of action.

She applauded as I played the finishing chord, and I discreetly slipped off my stool. While I was sitting there doing the song, I had, in fact, no way of confirming my worst fears, my guitar being between me and the problem. Calmly, I took a bow, acknowledging her approval, and at the same time taking a crafty look. All was painfully true. I turned to the band and walked to my amplifier as though to adjust the controls, then, in a flash (if you'll pardon the expression) all was put right. Returning to the mike I continued as my new found friend looked, then ate, then sipped her wine, then smiled.

Nowadays, I don't think that the same situation would cause so much embarrassment. We've all become so much more blasé and broad-minded about such things. And yet I doubt if there is a man who would honestly tell you that such an oversight would not make him feel uncomfortable. All I can say is, if it is going to happen to you, try not to be on the stage, sitting on a stool, singing a romantic song. It's the indignity of it all.

The Allegro Room downstairs was completely different, being patronised by a young 'debbie' sort of set. They talked and giggled all the time I was on. Not at my act, I hasten to add – they were just having fun amongst themselves and knocking back lots of 'champers'.

My final performance on the Saturday night was chaotic. A party of some twenty or so teenagers were having a whale of a time celebrating somebody's birthday. Just as I was pouring my heart out in some ballad or another, they chose that precise moment to burst forth in several different keys: 'HAPPY BIIIIRTHDAY DEAR CAROLIIIINE ... HAPPY BIRTHDAY TOOOO YOOOU.' They concluded their vocal tribute to Caroline just as I sang the closing lines of my song. A ripple of applause from the audience mingled with the raucous good wishes for the birthday girl. Having waited for a suitable lull in the proceedings, I began to introduce my next offering.

Suddenly from the furthest corner of the room

boomed a loud, husky and instantly recognisable Cockney voice.

''Ere, he's bloody good this bloke . . . wot ya say 'is name was?' The entire room turned to see who was making the row.

'Eh, Val wot?' he continued, oblivious to the attention he was getting. I envied his ability to achieve such silence, and wished at that moment I could be in the audience watching him instead of the other way around. It was one of my favourite comedians, Jimmy Wheeler. When I thought of the countless occasions I had stood in the wings of provincial theatres watching him in action I felt ashamed of my longing to ask him to shut up.

''Ere, quiet, you lot,' he bellowed at the gaping patrons. 'Give the man a chance . . . now belt up.'

A deathly hush fell on the room and I picked up where I had left off. The remainder of my act was a joy by comparison. Even Caroline's party gave me a hearing. In fact the only interruption I suffered was from dear Jimmy, who continued to shout his approval of my efforts. I was delighted to have a chat with him afterwards: he'd 'had a few', but his genuine concern for a fellow performer was heartwarming.

As I've said previously, these weekly engagements in London were few and far between and I was content most of the time with the odd 'one night stand'.

Some little time before I'd had a phone call from a band leader friend of mine. He was doing a regular weekend 'gig' at an Irish ballroom in the Shepherds Bush area, where on Saturday and Sunday evenings he played for dancing.

'If you ever feel like keeping your hand in at reading guitar parts, there's a job for you,' he told me. 'I can't pay you a lot of money, though,' he pointed out. 'It'll be five pounds a night.' There was nothing in the book at the time except for the radio show and I needed to stay in London to pursue my arranging work.

'I'll try it next week,' I said. 'I can play guitar and do a few vocals.'

'Great,' my friend Aiden said. 'I'll pick you up at seven o'clock, we might as well travel together.' The ten pounds I got every weekend for the next couple of months Lynn and I used to cover our mortgage payments. It was great fun and the experience did me no harm at all.

The manager of the ballroom was an Irish lad named Nelius O'Connell. We were to become very good friends and still are today. We were chatting one evening before the patrons arrived, discussing the success of the dance halls in Ireland at the time, and the emergence of the showband era. These bands started a whole new trend in dancing in the early sixties, concentrating as they did on entertaining the patrons as well as supplying the music. Several members of each group would get up and sing in their turn, covering all the different songs from the current charts and giving the people a kind of non-stop floor-show. Competition was quite fierce and the standard of entertainment had to improve all the time. The result was that the ballrooms competed in turn to acquire their services, and business boomed.

'By the way,' Nelius said, as I prepared to get on with my work, 'I could probably fix you a little tour over there if you like.' I sat down again for a minute. 'I won't be able to get you much money, though.' (I'd learned that this little proviso was par for the course.) 'But you'll get the chance to visit your family and make a few extra quid. I won't want any commission or anything.' (I was to learn also that *this* little proviso was *not* par for the course.)

I agreed to do about ten guest appearances around

Ireland, travelling from one town to another in my car. My fee was £25 a night.

The tour certainly wasn't a great success from the management's point of view, since most of the clientèle were very young people and didn't know me from Adam.

You may be somewhat alarmed or at least surprised to read of people in Ireland not knowing who Val Doonican was, so I'll try to explain. I spent the first four or five years of my professional life at home, working in Irish dance bands, travelling the length and breadth of the country before finally settling in Dublin. By the end of the forties, I'd reached the dizzy heights of having my own programme on Irish radio, but began to feel that it was time to seek pastures new. In the early fifties I moved to London and joined an Irish singing group called the Four Ramblers, who were working at the BBC (you may remember a Sunday afternoon radio series called *Riders of the Range*, which was very popular at the time and turned out to be my first job in England.) From then until the time in question some ten years had elapsed. I was forgotten by that radio audience back in Ireland, and had simply become the fellow with the guitar who stands on the left of the Four Ramblers.

Now my only claim to fame was a radio show every Thursday morning on the BBC Light Programme, which may have been listened to by a number of people in Ireland. Most of the people I came face to face with in Irish ballrooms were either at school, at work or listening to Radio Eireann while I did my stint on Tuesdays. In spite of falling between two stools I nevertheless enjoyed my mini tour back on my old stomping ground.

My radio work was beginning to bring in quite a batch of fan mail, a totally new experience for me. I got a strange kind of childish pleasure out of the fact that people were anxious to know what I looked like. I hadn't reached the 'autographed photo' stage yet, so I suggested that maybe listeners would like to write describing their own particular mental picture of me. Some of the letters were quite hilarious and I thoroughly enjoyed reading them out each week. To some I was tall and dark with curly hair. To others, short, fat and jolly. Several housewives thought I must be quite old and sport a beard: 'I'll bet you're a kind of Irish Burl Ives,' wrote one lady. She then went on to suggest that if I was young and handsome, I wouldn't sing songs like *Delaney's Donkey*. I made great capital of those letters which flattered me, assuring the writers that they were 'getting warm'.

I was receiving quite a lot of letters from listeners saying, 'We very much enjoy your choice of songs, they're very different, have you made any records?' Needless to say I had to reply in the negative. Recording contracts for singers of my particular style were at that time, as my old Dad would say, 'as scarce as hen's teeth'. Tapes of my radio show in hand, I hawked my wares around the various record companies, having first managed to acquire a few interviews with 'the powers that be', or should I say 'the powers that were at that particular time'. They were all very sympathetic, but totally honest in telling me that there wasn't much call for my kind of work on record. They quoted all the many people on their books, much more successful than I was, whose record sales left much to be desired.

'So,' one of them had asked me, 'what do you think you have got that so and so hasn't got?'

What can you say to that kind of argument?

'I don't know,' I answered, shrugging my shoulders. 'Maybe it's the fact that I'm me and he's him.'

Anyway, the answer was always the same: 'Sorry, but no thanks.' Quite honestly, I understood the logic of their reasoning, so I had to content myself with the fact that if I became more popular I might be able to force their hands a bit. I have a strong belief that there are many major considerations when trying to assess the prospects of a record's success. Some sell on the strength of the musical content, others on novelty value, others still sell because of the sheer popularity of the artist or artists concerned. Take for instance the signature tune from a show on television, or the recent phenomenon 'The Kids from Fame'. If their records had come out before the television shows, they might well have gone unnoticed. I'm sure that the many millions of albums I've been fortunate enough to sell did so because a lot of people wanted some sort of memento of what they enjoyed on my television shows.

A young West Indian told me this was called a 'lablolly' tree

—— Chapter Two ——

Let me take you back briefly to the early fifties, in order that I might introduce you to some very special people in my life.

When I arrived in London to join the Four Ramblers, I was promptly thrown in at the deep end of the Music Hall. Week after week we trudged about the country going from one provincial theatre to another to appear on various variety bills.

We never achieved any major recognition as a 'Top Of The Bill' act over the years, but even though I say it myself, we took a bit of beating when it came to closing the first half of the show. Thank goodness our services were called upon to perform that function with sufficient regularity to keep us all away from the dreaded Labour Exchange. Looking back we closed the first half, and I hope paved the way, for such notables of that period as Jimmy James, Norman Evans and Max Wall, not to mention 'youngsters' like Frankie Howerd and David Whitfield.

It was always considered a real prize to be invited by a promoter to support one of these celebrities for a whole tour. Since it was customary to work each town for an entire week, this kind of offer could keep you going for weeks, or even months. I hadn't been with the Ramblers long before such an offer came along. It involved an extensive tour with a show called *The Radio Party*, starring two real veterans of the British Music Hall, Morris and Cowley.

Harry Morris and Frank Cowley (they took their name from the old car Morris Cowley) were brothers, and married to two sisters Edith and Doris. Harry and Edith, or Chubby as she was affectionately known, had a daughter, Peggy, and they travelled everywhere together as a family. Peggy was a singer, but it was in the capacity of company manager, compère, and a 'comedian's labourer' that she worked with *The Radio Party*.

There certainly was a real family atmosphere among the resident cast of this particular company. We travelled as one, all assembling at the local railway station each Sunday morning, where we'd help to load our equipment aboard and head for the next venue. Some weeks our ranks would be augmented by a 'special guest', giving the whole thing a boost at the box office. These guests, I recall, ranged from such seasoned campaigners as Monsewer Eddie Gray, of the Crazy Gang, to a young, or should I say very young, lad named Des O'Connor. (And that was thirty years ago . . . Oh Des, what have I done?)

Harry, Chubby and Peggy befriended me since I seemed to be the only one who didn't dash off to the bar between entrances. I'd sit in my dressing room knowing full well that within minutes of the fall of the curtain a gentle tapping on the door would announce that 'tea was brewed'. I'd then retire to Number One and become one of the family.

Yes, we were to become such close friends that on our periodic sojourns back in London, I'd spend at least a couple of evenings a week at their flat in Peckham. This relationship blossomed through the fifties, and indeed continued long after I'd left the group. In fact when I took my first tentative steps into a solo career, it was Harry who kindly performed the temporary duties of personal manager and professional advisor. He secured auditions, interviews and later broadcasts for me, always offering to come along with me should I need any moral support. His performing days were nearing an end, but in spite of his very demanding commitment as secretary of the Grand Order of Water Rats, he gave me all the time and attention I needed. Peggy was by now (in addition to her own career) my part-time and unpaid assistant, attending to my business affairs.

Eventually things began to look promising for me, and Harry could see that it was time to do something about it.

'I don't think you need me any more, son,' he announced across the dinner table. 'The time has come to get yourself signed up with a well-established agent.'

He even came along to my first appointment with Eve Taylor, and continued to keep a fatherly eye on me, right up to his death in 1972. By now, however, Peggy had become an indispensable part of my work. As anybody who has ever tried to get in touch with me will know, she still rules the roost. By the way, the Morris and Cowley's real family name was Birkenhead.

Right through my working years with the Ramblers, I'd learned, more out of necessity than from any kind of musical inspiration, to supply whatever musical backing we needed. For the modest club and cabaret work in London I wrote out accompaniments for piano, organ, bass and drums plus the odd front line parts for trumpet, sax and so on. Within our own circle of professional friends I gained the misguided, if rather flattering, reputation of being a bit of a whizz kid with the music.

Our business affairs at that time were in the hands of Syd Royce, who in my eyes, at least, was a caricature of the typical Jewish agent. He was short, plump, very bald, and spoke with a rich Jewish accent. He organised our working lives from behind a desk in his tiny office in Charing Cross Road.

Syd rang me one day and asked if I could do him a favour. He'd taken under his wing a young comedian/impressionist, still in his teens, and was anxious to try him out in a few cabaret rooms in town. The young 'hopeful' had 'got his act together' and needed some music. I was offered the sum of eight pounds for the job, and it was arranged that I'd pop along to the office some days later, and see what could be done. A few laughs were in store as I mounted the rickety steps to Syd's tiny place of business above a music store. The young Peter Kaye was already there, bubbling with enthusiasm and sounding more like a fellow just about to open in Las Vegas. He wore a very smart suit, neat white shoes and his pièce de resistance, the very latest thing in trilby hats, à la 'Ol Blue Eyes' himself.

I took a seat, my guitar to hand for checking keys, etc, plus a few sheets of music manuscript and a well-sharpened pencil. It was high summer at the time, and in spite of the fact that all the office windows were wide open, it was stifling hot, and dear old Syd mopped his bald pate incessantly.

He couldn't wait for me to see what his young 'find' had in store.

'Go on, son,' he encouraged, 'show him the open-

31

ing. . .' then turning to me . . . 'This is sensational.'

'What's the first song?' I enquired, wanting to write something at the top of the page.

'*Mack the Knife*,' they both said in unison. Syd turned to the lad:

'Go out on to the landing, son, then you can make a proper entrance.'

Peter buttoned up his jacket, adjusted his precious hat to its most jaunty angle, then, giving the brim a final flick with his fingers, disappeared on to the tiny landing. After a short pause filled with expectancy, he began shouting instructions to me as to what the introduction should be.

'Barrah bah rahbah pow,' he sang, sounding like a one man impression of the entire Nelson Riddle Orchestra playing the intro. The door burst open, and he leaped into the room, clicking his fingers in tempo.

'Oh the shark has . . . Barah bah.' This was accompanied by a few fancy movements . . . 'Pretty teeth deah . . . Parah Pow.'

I sat there, pencil poised, wondering where all those imaginary brass figures were to come from when Nelson Riddle was substituted by a badly played piano and drums. Peter stopped.

'Now, at this point,' he said, 'I take off the hat and send it flying into the wings.' There followed a demonstration which sent Syd and I into roars of laughter, and poor Peter into a fit of depression.

'Parah. . .Pow,' he repeated, removing the hat and, with a sophisticated flourish, he sent it flying like a 'frisby' across the tiny office. Sadly, in his state of ecstasy, he'd forgotten that all the windows were open. Away went the brand new hat, sailing out over Charing Cross Road, landing like a flying saucer on the roof of a passing trolley bus, never to be seen again.

Peter went on to find great success in television and

theatre, and now lives with his family in Sydney, Australia. In fact, he interviewed me on television a few years ago, and the story of his new hat was the highlight of our get together.

My own first appearance on the West End stage was a strange one indeed. It took place back in the mid fifties, not, incidentally, in front of a regular theatre audience, but to a completely empty theatre. It took the form of a rather demoralising audition.

The Four Ramblers were given the chance of putting their talent on the line, one sunny afternoon, by accepting an audition for the privilege of appearing in an important summer show. The impresario on that occasion was none other than the ex-bandleader and stalwart of the entertainment world at the time, Jack Hylton. The chosen place of execution was to be the stage of the gigantic London Coliseum.

We arrived, eager and much too early, having rehearsed our party piece for days and nights on end. The selected sample of our wares, by the way, included an array of vocal group impressions, with a strong comedy element; at least, that's what we thought. I should mention that, in fact, we never actually had the pleasure of meeting Mr Hylton, a short, stocky man with grey hair, rimless spectacles, and sporting a hearing aid.

At three thirty we stood in the wings, as a solitary microphone awaited us, centre stage, in the white circle of the spotlight. A few rows back in the stalls sat the great man, his glasses glinting in the reflected light, his hearing aid placed firmly in position, his hands, in which we had placed our hopes, fiddling with a neatly folded newspaper.

At last we settled ourselves round the microphone. I played the introduction on my guitar. Ahead of us lay our well-rehearsed tribute to the Mills Brothers, the Four Freshmen, the Inkspots, the Four Lads. Early encouragement came from the sight of Mr Hylton tapping his daily newspaper against his knee in time with the music. We looked at each other and winked. Three vocal groups later, however, the winking had stopped, as one of our lads nodded towards the stalls. There sat our would-be employer, his newspaper now open and propped against the seat in front. He was reading. Then as we desperately tried to inject a last bit of enthusiasm into our impression of the 'Compagnons de la Chanson' singing *Little Jimmy Brown*, came the unkindest cut of all. Slowly Mr Hylton raised his free hand and removed the hearing aid.

This kind of indignity was less frequent now, and 1963 had been an eventful year for the Doonicans. Our home in Lee Green in south east London was our pride and joy. Lynn and myself had tackled all the 'newlywed' kind of chores. We had built in the kitchen cabinets, fitted a new sink unit complete with plumbing, rubber-tiled the floor, tiled the bathroom walls. Lynn had made the curtains and bed covers while I painted doors and windows, and papered the walls. Our little girl Siobhan had been born in July and made life complete.

My career, in the capable hands of Eve Taylor, was coming along in leaps and bounds. The cabaret dates were coming in and it looked as if the lad was on his way. 1964 began much the same, but then, alas, tragedy. We had to suffer the sad death of our daughter. She was discovered dead in her cot at about ten o'clock one evening. I'm sure that only people who have suffered the horrors of a 'cot death' could imagine what life became for us. The baby, the house, my career were all at once replaced by a kind of emptiness. Lynn was just wonderful and showed amazing strength of character.

Whenever tragedy struck my young life, my mother would come to the rescue with one of her favourite sayings, 'Never mind, love . . . God never closes one door but he opens another.' God was at that moment in our lives preparing to open not only a door, but the proverbial floodgates.

I could feel those first waves of success in the air somehow; my phone was constantly ringing with people I hardly knew asking me to take part in this and that . . . 'Would you like to do a guest spot on the Rolf Harris radio show?' or 'When you're in Manchester in a few weeks' time, how about doing a guest spot with the NDO?' The BBC Northern Dance Orchestra under its then conductor Alyn Ainsworth was probably the best known broadcasting band at that time. They had starred in an enormously successful television programme – which they previously did on radio – called *Make Way For Music*. It was a band show in the true sense, featuring wonderful arrangements by such stalwarts as Alan Roper, Pat Nash and members of the orchestra like Syd Lawrence, who now fronts his own very famous band. The show was introduced in a lovely humorous style by the witty Roger Moffatt who created most of his script at the expense of the band, the conductor, the producer, and of course, the poor vocalists Sheila Buxton and Roberto Cardinalli. Another member of the band who should be mentioned here is flautist Bernard Hermann. He was to take over the baton from Alyn Ainsworth, and was until recently to be seen on your television screens, in appropriate costume, directing the pit orchestra for the very popular *The Good Old Days*.

They were regular broadcasters doing their own show on radio and working as the resident orchestra on many light entertainment projects put out by the

BBC. The ones I took part in were mainly at lunchtime, *Midday Music Hall*, or *Easy Beat*.

Similar type shows were going out in London at the Playhouse Theatre on the embankment, one of the more popular of which was *Parade of the Pops*, featuring the music of Bob Miller and the Millermen. It had much the same formula as the Manchester show with popular singers, male and female, coming along as guests.

And so my date book began to fill up and my bank balance did likewise. I still look back over the years, you know, and ask myself why things happen at a particular time for no particular reason. Now people wanted me to take part in various programmes, doing precisely the same material they had turned down the year before.

I'm sure you'll recall the old *Tonight* shows on BBC back in the fifties with Cliff Michelmore, Alan Whicker, Fyfe Robertson, Derek Hart and many others. One of the regular features of the nightly transmissions was a closing song, to guitar accompaniment, from people like Cy Grant, Robin Hall and Jimmy McGregor or Noel Harrison. I managed to obtain an audition and went alone. I sang a cross-section of the little ditties which I was later to feature in my radio shows with great success. At that time, on that day, for some reason, they were not right for the show. Now some four or five years later I was accepted as a safe bet. It really is a weird and wonderful way to make a living.

In the end, 1964 turned out to be a memorable year for Val Doonican. It all happened, as they say, and in a big way. In fact, so hectic did things become that I find it difficult to look back and put it all in sequence.

A BBC television producer named Travers Thorneloe was given the task of putting together a short series of musical shows which he entitled *Singalong*

Saturday. Those two words, in fact, sum up the shows: they were transmitted on Saturday nights, the musical content was very much in the singalong category, and I was invited to be the host, introducing the items and leading the singing. I was to be joined on the set by the Adams Singers of *Sing Something Simple* fame, plus a small group of musicians. The audience was in vision, and sat in a semicircle of raised seats, in front of my little podium. It was all very new to me, and I loved every minute of it. I included many of my own style of songs, which I chose with great care, endeavouring when possible to have a little chorus where everybody joined in. I can't honestly say whether the whole thing was in any way successful, but I certainly must have made the right impression from the BBC's point of view, because it led to other things.

Also, about that time, a Manchester-based producer named John Ammonds was doing a series called *Barn Dance*, from the Dickenson Road studios in Manchester. He'd noticed some of my efforts on radio and television and contacted me, suggesting that we should meet and have a chat. On his next visit to London, we met in the basement canteen at Broadcasting House and, over a cup of BBC tea, we discussed the possibility of my doing a guest appearance on *Barn Dance*. My kind of songs with guitar accompaniment were ideal as far as John was concerned, and he booked me for about six appearances. At that time I had no idea how important my relationship with John would be to my future career.

He was one of the busiest producer/directors in the north, having had much success with such shows as the Harry Worth series, and several stints with the late Michael Holliday. *Barn Dance* was not, as one might immediately assume, a programme of country and western music, but was inspired more by the music of Northumbria. It featured a troupe of country dancers, a traditional dance band specialising in that kind of folk music, and a wide range of guests. The studio at 'Dickie Road', as it was affectionately known, was decked out to look like an old farm building, complete with bales of straw, farm implements and cart wheels, strewn about the place. There was a loft above the main set area, where some of the boys and girls would perch, their legs dangling over the edge. The show was hosted by a local lad, the well-known journalist and broadcaster Brian Redhead, whose voice we now hear every morning presenting the *Today* show on Radio Four. I shared the solo honours with such people as Steve Benbow, the Barrie Sisters and on one occasion Roger Whittaker. Needless to say, everybody wore casual clothes in keeping with the setting, the dancing girls sporting pretty summer dresses and the lads wearing check shirts. Lynn looked around the shops and found me some casual things for my wardrobe. Since I tended to look best in those kind of outfits anyway, the Doonican Sweater tag was soon established and became firmly associated with my television personality.

Just about then, the tragic news of the death of singer Michael Holliday shocked the entertainment world. Mike was, I suppose, the first of our home grown casual entertainers, although from what I gather he found the whole business of performing in public quite a strain. However, he did what he did very well and paved the way for people like myself.

It was at this time that a series of events led to the most important television spot of my career, at the London Palladium. I've already written about this in *The Special Years*, so let me quote from that to explain what happened.

David Jacobs was organising a big charity concert at the De La Ware Pavilion, Bexhill-on-Sea, and had asked me to appear on a bill which included Vera Lynn, Dickie Henderson, Frankie Vaughan and a host of others. I was delighted. My spot went well and Dickie Henderson was kind enough to come to my dressing room afterwards and pay me the first compliment I'd ever had from a celebrity.

'If you're not a star this time next year,' he said, 'there's no justice in show business.'

The following week I was booked to do a week's cabaret at the Piccadilly Club in Manchester city centre and one of the things I had to do, before making the trip, was to have my hair cut. It was my usual practice to have it done at the barber's shop in the Piccadilly Hotel in London whenever I was in town and I rang the barber, Jack Lee, and went in on the Wednesday.

While Jack was cutting my hair and we were indulging in the usual hairdresser-customer chit chat, he suddenly changed the subject, 'Oh! by the way,' he said, looking at me in the mirror, 'I had a fan of yours in here yesterday.'

'Really,' I replied. 'Who was it, Marilyn Monroe?'

'No, seriously,' said Jack waving his comb about, 'it was Dickie Henderson – said he was going to tell Val Parnell about you – loved your act on Sunday night.' So, it wasn't the old flannel, he did mean it!

It was at that stage that things began to fall into place. The very next day the man sitting in that barber's chair was, in fact, Val Parnell – probably the greatest impresario this country had and the man responsible for, among other things, the TV show *Sunday Night at the London Palladium*. As Jack was cutting his hair, he related the story about Dickie and myself. Mr Parnell said he hadn't heard of me but showed interest.

As for me, I went off to Manchester at the weekend and booked into my digs for the week. The manager of the club, Jerry Harris, quite staggered me, midweek, by telling me that a gentleman named Alec Fyne was in town and would be popping in for a few minutes. Now this particular gentleman, believe it or not, happened to be Val Parnell's talent scout and booking manager and, at that time, knew absolutely nothing about the 'barber's shop quartet'. He sat and watched me, while he ate and had a drink and, afterwards, sent me his compliments.

Next day, on his return to London, he mentioned me to Val Parnell who, by now, was becoming sufficiently interested to ask where I was working next, in case he decided to come and have a look for himself.

The following week was perfect: I was at 'The Jack of Clubs', a restaurant owned by a family called Isow, which was situated right in the heart of Soho. I was appearing there, once nightly, at about eleven fifteen. Somebody up there loved me again that week, for on Monday, Tuesday and Wednesday, the audience were not very interested but – on Thursday, they were wonderful. Mr Parnell chose to have a look at me on the Thursday.

My performance was as good as I could make it and I had nothing whatever to complain about. After I'd finished, I had a message that the great man wanted to speak to me. He was so charming to me and not at all like the impresarios you see in the movies – none of the 'I'm gonna make you a star' bit or anything like that, just a straightforward compliment. 'You were great tonight,' he said smiling, 'very refreshing stuff. I think you'd do well on *Sunday Night at the Palladium*.'

'What!' I said, sitting bolt upright. 'Are you serious?'

He turned to Alec Fyne who was with him at the table. 'What vacant dates have we got, Alec?' he asked.

After a quick flick through his diary, Alec Fyne suggested the last Sunday in May or the first Sunday in June.

Mr Parnell looked at me, 'What do you say, then?'

'Oh!' I said, 'yes, I can do both those Sundays.' It was meant to be a silly joke, from an embarrassed but very excited man. As it turned out – I did both those Sundays.

In fact, John Ammonds released me from one of my *Barn Dance* commitments in order that I might fulful the Palladium slot, knowing how important it could be to my career, since it had the highest viewing figures of any of the popular shows at that time. During previous weeks he had been discussing with me the possibility of doing a show of my own, so I was pleased in the knowledge that this single television success might swing things in the right direction for me.

Following my second appearance in two weeks, 'all hell broke loose'. Eve's phone was ringing constantly, people suggesting all sorts of things I might like to do. I sat in her office and threw my hands up in a kind of happy confusion.

'What do I accept and what do I refuse?' I asked her, never having had this kind of decision to worry about before.

'I'll tell you what to do,' Eve said quietly, and saying things quietly was not one of Eve's strong points. 'You'll do nothing. You and Lynn should pack a bag and go away for a few days and have a good chat about everything and leave all the hassle to me. The offers will still be there when you get back, so what's needed is time for us all to make the right decisions.'

That turned out to be one of the best pieces of advice I've ever had in my career. We didn't want to go too far from home, what with the other bookings I still had to fulfil. We decided to have a week in Jersey. The weather was quite good so we did as we were told, packed our bags and went.

I'd never been to Jersey before. Neither had Lynn for that matter, so we both looked forward to having a few relaxed days looking around the island. Our horizon looked bright indeed, the prospects for the coming year surpassing anything I might have foreseen only weeks previously. One of the Sunday papers sent a reporter and photographer (with our approval, I might add) to write a feature on our little retreat. They were amazed, but pleased from a story point of view, to discover that we had hired a couple of bicycles and intended to cycle around the countryside, taking in some fresh air and enjoying the scenery. The two lads were really great, getting the whole thing done in as short a time as possible, allowing us to have a bit of time together. They took some good photographs, and brought back what I hope was an interesting article. I've never really considered myself to be what the press call 'good copy'. Over the years, in spite of my considerable success, I've always felt that they found it difficult to make what they wrote about my activities sound all that interesting. In all my years as an entertainer, I've never had any kind of a press agent or publicity representative. I could never imagine what the poor guy would find to talk about.

Anyway, Lynn and I had a lovely week just being away from the usual household routine. We talked endlessly about what the future might hold for us. Deep down inside I had a strange feeling of not wanting to return too quickly, knowing I'd have to make some serious decisions, and having done so, carry out their consequences.

We came home on the Saturday night. Eve rang me on the Sunday asking me to drop into the office on Monday afternoon.

She was a very happy lady indeed, and wore a sort of smug expression, like somebody who knows things that they know you're dying to know. The next hour or so revealed an amazing change in my professional standing. There were offers for television shows of my own, several record contracts at our disposal, a choice of summer season shows, and weeks in cabaret at venues hitherto out of my depth. Eve sat back in her chair and smiled at me, looking pleased for both of us. She summoned it up with a phrase which was to become part of my life for years and years.

'Well, love,' she said, 'I'll tell you what I think you should do, and then you can do what you like.' Her tone of voice was reminiscent of my mother saying to me as a child, 'Well, love, you go out without a vest if you want to, but if you get double pneumonia, don't expect me to look after you.' Eve told me what to do, and I did it.

It was decided that firstly, I shouldn't sign any long term contracts with anybody if I could possibly avoid it, but try from a television point of view to secure one short series of half-hour shows which would enable me to feel my feet. I had little idea at this stage what kind of show I could handle, so making the wrong move, especially over too long a period, could ruin all the good which had been done. Both BBC and ITV had made approaches regarding the prospects of signing me up: this included the suggestion that I might try a stint of hosting the *Sunday Night at the London Palladium* show. The latter, Eve and I agreed, would be completely out of my reach, since my style was too intimate, and my experience in comparison to Bruce Forsyth and the other compères was negligible.

Secondly, any record contract which we signed should, if possible, be negotiated on a lease tape basis. This means that we would pay all the expense of having the record made, then having done so present the finished article to whichever record company offered us the best deal. The important element of this kind of contract is that whatever else happens to that tape through its life, it always remains the personal property of the people who made it originally. To this day I possess virtually every song I ever recorded, and nobody can release any recording of mine without first coming to me for the hire of the tapes. Since the number of titles run into hundreds, I owe an

Bananas and papayas

enormous debt of gratitude to Eve for her astute guidance at that time.

Eve concluded her good news and rose from her desk. 'Sorry love,' she apologised, 'I have to dash off for an appointment at the BBC. I'll sort everything out and come back to you. I'm seeing Tom Sloan and Bill Cotton in half an hour.' I came out into Regent Street and waved to Eve as she dashed off in a cab. It's hard to describe my feelings that day. Having worked on the factory floor of show business for such a long time, I now felt as though I'd been offered the job of Managing Director. It was great to drive home knowing I had such tasty news to pass across the dinner table.

In fact, Eve rang me back later that evening. She rounded my day off with the news that the BBC had agreed to let me do six shows. They were in complete harmony with our feelings that we should start small and get the thing right.

'They'd like you to do six shows from Manchester,' she told me. 'John Ammonds will be producing them, and the NDO will be resident orchestra.' This was exactly what I'd hoped for and I told her so. 'Good,' she said, 'I'll look into the record side tomorrow, so will you go through all the music and demos [these are demonstration records sent by songwriters] and I'll do the same and maybe we'll find something.'

After a few 'thank yous' and mutual congratulations I was just about to hang up when Eve shouted, 'Oh by the way, love,' and what a 'by the way' it turned out to be. 'With all the excitement of today's news I forgot to ask you, how would you like to top the bill at the London Palladium?' There was a pause, and then we both began to laugh. 'I'm serious,' she screamed, still laughing.

'Oh, come on Evie,' I said. 'If you're serious, why the hell are you fallin' about laughing?'

45

'Because I can just see your little face, that's why,'
then the serious Evie took over. 'Listen, Val, you
know Frankie Vaughan is doing a long season at the
Palladium at the moment. Well, in September, he's
got to take a night off because he doesn't work on the
Jewish feast of Yom Kippur and they want someone
to take over for the night.'

The prospect of topping a bill which included such
names as Tommy Cooper, Cilla Black, Peter Good-
wright and Audrey Jeans was enough to scare the
wits out of me, let alone the thought of trying to win
over a theatre full of Frankie Vaughan fans.

'You're joking,' I gasped, breaking the silence as
Evie waited. 'I'd die on my feet, although I'm sure I
should have a go. What do you think?' I knew what
was coming, she was 'going to tell me what she
thought, and then I was going to do what I liked.' She
did just that.

'I honestly don't think you are well known enough
to do it, but on the other hand, you're not well known
enough for it to do you any harm. I don't think you've
got anything to lose.'

That was all the encouragement I needed. 'I'll do it,'
I said.

The next week or so saw us wading through dozens
of songs with the idea of finding something which
might make an interesting single. One of the snags, if
I could describe it as such, was the fact that I wasn't
known for any particular type of song. I did standards, folk songs, Irish comedy numbers and material
which was popular at the time. What sort of thing was
I to choose? There was a little country-type song on a
demo sent by a publishing friend, Peter Callender,
then with Shapiro Bernstein Music, and the title of
this little song was *Walk Tall*. We finally settled for
that, and decided to use a thing called *Only the Heartaches* as a B side. (*Only the Heartaches* was yet another

adaptation of the old traditional ballad *The Streets of Laredo*.)

Arranger Ken Woodman had been doing some writing for another of Eve's artists, Chris Andrews, so it was decided that he and I would get together on the music. I arranged *Walk Tall* and Ken did *Heartaches*. As far as I can recall, the entire venture cost a few hundred pounds. I brought the finished product to Eve, and she went into action. After much to-ing and fro-ing she settled for Decca Records, who liked the disc, and my first single was born. It was to be a million seller.

I should add a little footnote to that last paragraph, for the benefit of those who might be familiar with my early recording activities. Another friend from the publishing world, Terry Oates, had, some time previously, offered through his employers, Chappell Music, to put up the money for me to make a record. We made what in those days was called an EP or extended player, a record with two titles on each side. Nothing very much came of that venture, but the record was released and turned out very well.

Walk Tall had just been released when my celebrated 'topping of the bill' at the Palladium coincided with preparations for my first television series. Life had become hectic for me and already I was beginning to know what the added responsibility of a degree of success felt like. People were talking about me and naturally more was expected of me than I was used to serving up.

Lynn, who had played dozens of times at the famous theatre herself, came along with Eve to boost my confidence at rehearsals. It was arranged that Tommy Cooper, who was appearing just before the star spot, would introduce me. The stage manager popped his head into my room, or rather Frankie Vaughan's room, and wished me luck. Minutes later, I stood behind those famous curtains waiting for the magic words from Tommy that would begin my ordeal.

'Ladies and gentlemen,' Tommy began, 'as you probably know from the notice in the foyer, Frankie Vaughan will not be appearing tonight.' There was a gasp of disappointment from the packed house, many of whom had obviously not seen the notice. 'However,' Tommy went on, 'we're fortunate to have a young man who is making quite a name for himself...' and so it went on for what felt like forever... 'So let's have a great big welcome tonight for...' There was a sickening pause. Tommy, bless him, obviously had no idea of my name... 'Here he is.' He then mumbled something that sounded like Halm Nillighen ... and walked off applauding.

I often look back on that night with feelings of absolute horror. There I was, facing the most important audience of my career, a theatre filled with visitors from all over the world. Not only were they disappointed at not seeing the show they'd paid to see, but they were faced with some fellow who had a name something like Halm Nillighen. Even my mother had never heard of him.

I smiled my way rather impatiently through the opening song, and then tried, with a certain amount of desperation, to explain my presence. I got through that evening somehow, although I don't think of the whole thing as much of a personal triumph. My act, I suppose, was still geared to the kind of club dates I was accustomed to, and required quite a bit of adjusting and polishing before I took it into such sophisticated surroundings. Anyway, it acted as yet another tug on my professional choke chain, and brought me to heel for a while.

John Ammonds and I had met several times by now to talk over the proposed format for the television series. I was to take over the slot left by the untimely death of Mike Holliday. He and Perry Como were undoubtedly the main influences in the general outline put forward. Like most people interested in entertainment, I was an avid viewer of the long running Perry Como shows through the fifties and sixties. One important difference, of course, was the fact that I was to have the orchestra in vision and indeed they were to be featured quite heavily in a solo capacity.

My show was, to be perfectly honest, a kind of trial-run and the budget was limited, so there was little chance of having any 'star guests' as such. The shows suffered very little as a result, I'm glad to say, and all the work put into making the most of what was at our disposal paid off handsomely.

We went on the air at 7.30 pm on Wednesday nights for our six week run. To put a newcomer on at such a time, competing as it was with the might of *Coronation Street* was, you may think, foolhardy. Whatever the reason may have been for its placing, it suited me just fine. I was able to learn my job of television host without too much responsibility as far as viewing figures were concerned. The outcome was, in fact, that the show was quite a success in its own modest way, and I was immediately booked for another series.

For one week in that first series my guest was a very attractive young Irish girl who was based in England. It was decided that we would sing something together, and then for her solo spot she would sing a little Irish lullaby. Having heard the song a few times, John Ammonds decided that it might look nice if she were to sing it sitting in a chair by a mock fireplace. A search party from among the scene crew was sent to scour the prop room situated probably somewhere in the bowels of the earth under the old church where we were rehearsing. Eventually, they returned with a black rocking-chair, which, having been cleaned and polished, was placed on its mark before the fire.

John now decided that the situation didn't allow for the use of the usual hand mike and asked the sound lads to have a small radio mike concealed down the front of the lady's dress. Once the mike had been secreted, rehearsals continued. Gently the young mother began to serenade her imaginary baby, only to be accompanied with each rock of the chair by a weird squeaking sound. Since the sound coincided with the movement of the rocking chair, the young lady was asked to move, and the rockers, the cushion, the arms and the headrest were scrutinised for 'squeaks'. The search was in vain, however, so we tried again. The squeak continued loud and clear and rehearsals stopped once more. John was getting a bit impatient by now, as time was running short and there was much to be done. He appeared through the studio door, hotfoot from his control room upstairs. There was great activity around the chair, while further investigations were carried out. At last, to everybody's relief, and to the young lady's slight embarrassment, the source of the problem was discovered. The trouble, it seemed, was the position of the radio mike. Nestling as it was in the comfort of her bosom, it was picking up some extraneous noises from the movement of her bra as she rocked back and forth. The mike was moved slightly one way, then the other, but alas, the squeaky bra continued to dominate the situation. By now, time was at a premium. John ordered the chair to be moved, the young lady to stand by the fireplace, and the song to be performed with feeling, and little movement, in a standing position. Everything was fine, so we broke for tea.

John and I sat in the corner of the canteen with his secretary, Sybil, and assessed the situation. So far, the show seemed to be coming along well.

'T'was a shame about the number in the chair,' John said, sipping his tea. 'It looked really nice in that pool of light, but the sound wasn't quite right, even without the squeaks.' He put his cup down and scratched his head. 'How about trying your ballad sitting in the chair? You could use a boom mike and get away with it.' I said that I was happy to go along with it if John thought it would work. Fifteen minutes later, we tried it out and the man upstairs was delighted with the result. 'Listen, mate,' he said, making a special visit to the studio, 'that looks really nice, in fact, I think we should finish the show on it.' Everybody looked in amazement. 'Finish a light entertainment show on a quiet ballad, sitting in a rocking chair?' was the general thought. 'I tell you, it's going to look great,' said John, 'take my word for it, I'm right.'

My goodness, how right can you be? Little did any of us know on that evening in the autumn of 1964, what a milestone in my career that old black chair would become. As the trilby hat and the pipe were to Crosby, or as Morecambe was to Wise, the rocking chair and myself have become synonymous. On many occasions, over the twenty or so series I've hosted, I've thought that maybe the time had come to get rid of the chair idea, fearing that people would find it too predictable. In each case the public reaction was such that I retrieved it from the attic, if only for an occasional airing.

A few years ago, while making an overnight stop at a hotel in Colombo, Sri Lanka, I went into the cocktail bar to pass away some of the time to be filled. A couple of bar stools away was a very handsome middle-aged Indian chap, dressed in the familiar 'all white strip' so common in that part of the world. He smiled politely as he caught my eye, then, almost immediately, he moved one stool along and began to chat.

'Good evening Sirrrrr,' he greeted me, in that beautiful Peter-Sellers-type accent, 'are you here on business?' I told him I was just passing through on my way to join my family in the Seychelles for a holiday. 'I get to see a lot of businessmen passing through here,' he informed me. 'I know their faces, you see, and I've seen *your* face before.' I smiled, convinced that he was either giving me a bit of old flannel, or confusing me with somebody else. He read the disbelief in my expression. With his eyes half closed, he pointed a finger at me as if trying to place me exactly. When he spoke, his face broke into a cheeky smile. 'I think by your face, sir, that you are the chairman.' The title was snapped out as if it were the answer to the sixty-four thousand dollar question.

I laughed out loud, thinking, 'The chairman of which company, may I ask? I must talk to them about my salary!'

His face changed now, but the finger still pointed. 'You are the chairman, sir ... the chairman ... *the chair man* ... The man who sits in the chair and sings.' I was flabbergasted. I discovered that he'd just got back from a spell in Singapore, where my shows were transmitted every week. So you see, the chair was just as important to him as I was myself.

I related the story about the origin of the rocking chair to a newspaper reporter in America some years ago. When, eventually, I saw it in print, the headline read: IRISH CROONER FINDS TELEVISION SUCCESS BY NOT WEARING A SQUEAKY BRASSIERE.

I'll never know what words were spoken in high places at the BBC about my initial efforts as a television personality, but news came through from Eve instructing me to go along for an appointment with Tom Sloan (who was Head of Light Entertainment at the time) and his assistant Bill Cotton Jnr.

Sitting in Head Office, complete with glass in hand, I was informed that they were pleased indeed with my work. Such was their enthusiasm, in fact, that they'd decided to move my next series to London the following year and hoped to make it a much more ambitious affair. They were quick to allay any fears I may have had about losing the now established working relationship I had with John Ammonds. He was, in fact, in the process of moving to London and would be in charge of things as before.

I'd never really fancied myself as a potential candidate for *Top of the Pops*, but suddenly it was a reality. *Walk Tall* was now showing in the charts, so Eve had a call from producer Johnnie Stewart asking if I could report to the studio for that week's edition of the show. My run-through was much later than intended due to the late arrival of some American group; the young audience was already filtering into the studio while the camera and lighting men tried to get their house in order.

Perched on a high metal stool, microphone in hand and patiently awaiting my cue to start the song, I glanced downward, coming face to face with two extremely young ladies both chewing bubble gum, a bewildered look on their eyes.

'Oo's he?' one said, nudging a passing stranger. 'Dunno,' he mumbled. Next she tried the floor manager: ''Ere, oo's he?' she repeated, pointing to me over her shoulder as if thumbing a lift.

'That's Val Doonican,' he shouted, then disappeared about his business.

'Wot did 'e say?' she asked her friend.

'Val sumfin', I fink. That's a girl's name.' Then taking one final look at me she sniggered, 'Well, 'ooever he is . . . he's not arf bleedin' old.' Well, I *was* nearly thirty-seven.

That was the first of many, many appearances I was

to make on this most successful show over the years.

We could see that *Walk Tall* was going to be a huge hit, so I set about preparing my first album. I'd gathered some songs together based on their popularity through the radio show. Strangely enough the final list amounted to thirteen titles.

'Do you think thirteen will be unlucky?' I asked Lynn.

'Well, I can't see any of those songs being anything but lucky for you up to now,' Lynn said. 'I'd do them all.' Since the songs were so varied, we decided on the title 13 *Lucky Shades of Val Doonican*. They were very lucky shades, too, taking the album right to the top of the charts.

Lynn was expecting our second child during this period, so she was pretty well confined to barracks. Our home in Lee Green had a certain emptiness about it since the death of our baby girl the previous year and we had spoken often about the possibility of making a move. Strictly from the practical side of my work, I'd always felt that we lived in the wrong part of London. The great majority of the clubs and theatres I was likely to play were in the Midlands, or further north, so I was constantly faced with a trip right through London. We had come to the conclusion that somewhere to the north-west of the city would be the solution.

We drew a circle on the map of the Greater London area, encompassing the start of the M1, the A1, the M4, the M3, London Airport and the BBC Television Centre at Shepherds Bush. We began our search one morning during the following week. Next day, I had to drive to London again to take part in a broadcast. During rehearsals I sat in the auditorium of the Playhouse Theatre chatting with Keith Fordyce, who hosted the programme each week.

'Lynn and I went house-hunting yesterday,' I said

casually, as we watched Kathy Kirby going through her paces on stage.

'Whereabouts are you looking?' Keith asked, sipping his coffee.

'Oh, around Northwood, Pinner and Rickmansworth,' I said. 'I thought it was very nice there, although we didn't see anything we really liked.'

Keith turned to me with a look of disbelief. 'You're looking for a house in Rickmansworth, and I'm trying to sell mine! We're wanting to buy a place nearby that has a small market garden, which is just what we'd like to have.'

Within minutes we'd arranged a viewing some days later. We loved the house the moment we saw it, and decided to have it. As always with house purchasing, the price was a bit more than we intended to pay, but things were looking good for me professionally, so we weren't too worried.

Eve assured us that offers of cabaret and personal appearances were coming in at fees well in advance of any I'd had previously, so we put our house up for sale.

Screw pine

—— Chapter Three ——

When the 1965 summer shows were being planned and allocated, my name became worthy of consideration for the first time. I wasn't competing for the 'up market' bookings, I might add – in fact, the offer which came my way concerned a theatre listed for demolition: the Palace Theatre on the Isle of Man. Believe it or not, the demolition men went into action during my last week there, covering over the evidence of their depressing task each evening with huge canvas sheets.

Again, the show wasn't a great success. It was still early days as far as my popularity and drawing power were concerned, and the venue couldn't have been described as a going concern. However, it was a good show and I was accompanied in my efforts by a very talented cast. It included singer Jackie Trent, the vocal quartet the Jones Boys, and a very funny young comedian, of whom I'll speak more in a moment.

The eventual move to our new home unfortunately

happened to coincide with the opening of my summer show, so Lynn, in spite of her 'condition', suggested staying at home and supervising matters while I got on with earning the money to pay for it. Each week, weather permitting, I would come to London to record my radio shows and attend to any other business matters, while at the same time popping home to see how things were coming along. Once the painters and decorators moved in, Lynn joined me on the Isle of Man for a well-earned rest.

Prior to the summer season I had done some cabaret work, including a week at one of the most successful night spots in the north-east, La Dolce Vita in Newcastle. Some old friends whom I'd known since my Rambler days lived in the area, and kindly invited me to spend the week with them. I was delighted to accept since I've never been a great lover of hotel life. I dropped my luggage there in the afternoon and made my way to the club for rehearsals. My supporting act was a name new to me; he had, in fact, just returned to Britain from Australia where he had been working with some success for a few years. He'd had his own television show there and we talked at great length about the pros and cons of trying to make a career in that particular medium.

Later that evening I stood in the shadows at the back of the room and watched him go through his paces, and what sure-footed paces they were. He really was a lovely artist to watch, and watch him I did each evening that week with great admiration. We said farewell after the Saturday night show and went our separate ways. I had no doubt in my mind that we were going to see a lot of that gentleman in the future.

One lunchtime when I returned from a round of golf at Castledown on the Isle of Man, there was a message in my room asking me to ring Bill Cotton at the BBC Television Centre in London. The ensuing conversation was to play a very important part in my career.

'Hello, mate,' Bill said. 'Hope I haven't dragged you away from your golf, but John Ammonds and I have been having a chat about your new series, which, incidentally, will be going out on Thursday nights "live" from the television theatre. Now I know that you've got the Adams Singers resident with you, but I feel that it would be a good idea to have some kind of regular comedy spot as well.' His idea was that instead of finding a different comedian each week, it would be better to have someone whom the viewers could get to know and accept as part of the weekly format. 'Now, I think I know just the lad to fit the bill,' Bill assured me enthusiastically. 'He's had lots of television experience, but he has not been over-exposed in this country.' Then to my amazement and great pleasure he mentioned my new-found friend from La Dolce Vita in Newcastle. I agreed without hesitation. That partnership was to last for several years and contribute greatly to the show's popularity. It was inevitable that the man was to go on to great things, as he certainly did. His name was Dave Allen.

Strangely enough the other comedian with whom I shared the summer months was to become another of our stalwarts in the years that followed. I remember sitting with him and his wife in their little apartment, and listening to his disenchantment with his lack of success. He even spoke of giving it all up if things didn't show signs of improving. I'll bet he's glad he didn't now. It was Les Dawson. One thing is certain about this great world of entertainment, you've got to take the good and the bad as they present themselves, otherwise you're in the wrong job.

One of the items in our summer extravaganza was a duet featuring Jackie Trent and myself. Our young producer was evidently a fan of the old Hollywood-type musicals, and suggested this number in the first place. The stage was swathed in white drapes, its sole furnishing being a white grand piano. I stood in the well of the instrument dressed in a white tuxedo and black dress trousers. Jackie, who incidentally plays piano very well, sat at the piano in a flowing black evening gown. The song chosen for our rather out-of-character offering was the old standard *So In Love With You Am I*. The producer, who had obviously waited all his life for this opportunity, decided to complete his little moment of self-indulgence by slowly covering the stage with a 'dry ice' effect, giving the overall impression that Jackie and I were floating in the clouds. Well, I'm sure this sort of thing is fine when it features Fred Astaire and Ginger Rogers, and when the staging is in the hands of Busby Berkeley, but we had no such luck. Looking back, I'm sure poor Jackie must have hated every minute of it: it wasn't her scene at all. The weather was very hot and humid, so in order to make the whole evening bearable, doors had to be left open, including the scenery doors behind the stage. The fresh air was a godsend to everybody in the building, but alas, it didn't do a lot for our dry ice effect. As Jackie and I gazed into each other's eyes across the piano, the machine was switched on and the clouds merging from the wings slowly enveloped our legs, wafting us into our imaginary paradise. However, that gentle evening breeze coming through the back doors sent the sky floating away from beneath our feet and towards our startled audience. Seconds later, as we turned to deliver our romantic message . . .

> Strange dear, but true dear,
> When I'm close to you dear,
> The stars fill the sky,
> So in love with you am I . . .

...we were faced with the astonishing sight of an auditorium covered in a low cloud with hundreds of grinning faces peeping through the top. Jackie was the first to go, bursting into hysterical laughter while I gallantly carried on singing the harmony line to a non-existent melody. Eventually, I too crumbled, the entire thing finishing in complete chaos. The orchestra, which was by now absolutely invisible, bravely stuck to their task of supplying the ghostly accompaniment, little knowing what was happening above the clouds.

I returned from the Isle of Man at the end of that summer of 1965 filled with anticipation of an exciting autumn ahead. There was my television series, now scheduled to be screened at peak viewing time, following the nine o'clock news on Thursday evenings; the pleasure of settling into our new house; but most of all there was the joy of doing so accompanied by our newly born daughter, Sarah Louise. Her arrival just about coincided with my return, so it was indeed a family homecoming.

Our brand new home was beautiful, Lynn's interior decor giving it a warm, homely feeling. She's always had the most amazing talent for interior design and her taste and perception in colour scheme are always impressive. There is little doubt that had she not found her success in the world of the theatre, she could have had a professional career in this field. Our present home in Buckinghamshire is evidence to that, as I'm sure our friends will agree.

Sarah was a lovely child and brought us much happiness in those days as Lynn and I dashed about, coping with our newly found responsibilities. The press were constantly visiting the house to acquire publicity shots of the new arrivals: Sarah's into the world, and mine into the limelight.

Plans for the series were now taking place almost daily with John, Dave Allen, the Adams singers, the Gojos (a quartet of very attractive and talented young dancers who were to be part of the regular line-up of the series ... they were the creation of choreographer Jo Cook, and remained with me for many years), set designers, musical arrangers, costume supervisors and anybody else involved. Right from the start I've always been keen to know what's going on, even in those early planning stages. I do believe that if the show has your name on it, and you intend going on the air 'live', then it's wise to know as much as you can about all aspects of it. Lynn agreed to take the responsibility of finding all the casual wear which, even by now, had become a kind of trade mark of mine. The BBC included the extra money in my fee and then left the choice of clothes to us. The sweaters were a constant source of conversation, and my mail was laden with enquiries as to where such and such a jumper could be acquired. Contrary to popular rumour, incidentally, I was not flooded with knitwear from admiring fans. Virtually every piece of casual wear I used over the years was the result of endless shopping. The myth that little old ladies all over the land were sitting in rocking-chairs by their firesides furiously getting next week's wardrobe finished was a figment of the imagination of the popular press. I *was* sent gifts of knitwear from time to time, but strangely enough they were always unsuitable for some reason or another. Such was the impact created by my ever-changing collection that even today I'm constantly receiving requests for knitted donations to various charities. I haven't worn the sweaters for years now, so the drawers, I regret to say, are empty, except for my golfwear. That closing line was inserted at the request of my secretary, who has to answer the above mentioned letters.

The show's format took shape, at least on paper, and included such regular items as a four minute spot from Dave Allen, a speciality type number from the choir and me, a dance routine from the Gojos and a little 'chat' interlude from me, followed by a song with the guitar. The item with the Adams Singers became very popular indeed, and each week BBC script editor John Law and myself would set some time aside to work on it, John writing the words which I would then set to music. I found John to be a brilliant man with words: his inspiration seemed inexhaustible. Even today I sometimes read some of our early creations and marvel at his originality and sense of humour. Sadly, he died in the late sixties and was a great loss to the scriptwriting world.

Our thirteen week series was well received by the public and the critics alike, and established me as part of the television scene from then on. Dave's impact was inevitable and his fast growing band of followers eagerly awaited his weekly interlude. As I previously mentioned, his spot in the show was a mere four minutes, but it proved to be sufficient time for him to win over the audience. There were weeks I remember when that entire allocation of time was devoted to telling one simple joke, a technique he's developed with great skill as we can see from his work today.

Choosing a follow-up to *Walk Tall* was a difficult task. I often think that your second single can be more important than the first since you have so much to lose. The first release is invariably 'in the lap of the Gods', whatever your standing in the business, but the follow-up will decide whether you can really establish your position as a recording success. The temptation, of course, is to find a similar kind of song to your original. After much heart-searching, Eve and I felt we should risk something completely different. The same publishers who had sent *Walk Tall* came up with a ballad called *The Special Years*, written by an American lady named Martha Sharpe. This was released in the autumn of 1965 and immediately entered the charts. With the help of the popularity of the television series it was soon in the top three.

My inclusion in that year's edition of BBC's *Christmas Night with the Stars* ended a memorable year for the Doonican household. Life being what it is, however, I wasn't going to be allowed to have ideas above my station. As I've said before, show business has that happy knack of bringing you back down to earth. On my way to the studio to rehearse my contribution to the Christmas celebrations I paused to pop into a tobacconist's shop on the A40.

'Good morning,' I said, rubbing my hands together, the weather outside being somewhere around zero. 'Could I have a two ounce tin of Balkan Sobranie pipe tobacco please.'

The gentleman behind the counter looked up from his morning paper.

'Certainly, sir,' his voice tailed off as he caught my eye, he looked for a second or so and then shook his head. 'Sorry, mate,' he said apologetically, 'I know it's rude to stare, but you're an absolute dead ringer for that Val Doonican bloke on the telly.'

It was my turn to smile now. 'Yeah, I know,' I answered, 'lots of people have told me that lately.'

He reached on to a shelf behind him and produced my tin of tobacco. Still sniggering to himself he then said, 'What a pity the wife isn't here this morning, we could have had one over on her.'

I slipped the tin into my pocket. 'Why do you say that?' I asked him.

'Well,' he said, 'she'll never miss that bloke, she thinks he's marvellous,' then shaking his head in disbelief he added, 'I can't stand the bugger myself.' As we both had a laugh at Val Doonican's expense he said with a glint in his eye, 'Mind you, I wouldn't mind having a bit of his money.'

I stretched out my hand. 'Well there's a quid of it for a start.' I laughed this time as he handed me some change. I said cheerio, wished him a Happy Christmas and left. As I sat in my car preparing to pull out into the passing traffic I looked back to see a puzzled face gazing out between the chocolate boxes in the window. The joke at this stage was on both of us.

I've been a pipe smoker on and off since my early twenties, my introduction to the questionable habit having come about more through following a current fashion than by any kind of addiction. I'd entered into the Dublin danceband scene at the time when young men-about-town, influenced by movie stars of the suave kind, thought pipe smoking looked pretty smooth.

My first 'instrument', as it were, was a cheap little thing with a small bowl which got frightfully hot and kept going out every five minutes. The tobacco I chose didn't help either, although I didn't get through very much. It was the matches that cost me a fortune.

Among the musicians who were working colleagues at the time, was a piano player named Jimmy Banks. You always knew when Jimmy was about by the beautiful aroma of tobacco from his stout, professional-looking 'model'. I envied his ability to sit for what seemed like hours, gently puffing away as he played, a trickle of blue smoke appearing to emanate from the top of his head. Because Jimmy was a piano player, I usually saw his back, the pipe only coming into my view when I played the occasional 'bum' note and he turned to scowl at me. Try as I might to copy his technique, my pipe continued to burn my tongue, make horrible squelching noises, go out after the first chorus of each tune we rehearsed, and smell like old gum shoes.

Eventually the whole thing came to a head when Jimmy, growing increasingly intolerant of my onslaught upon the reputation of 'proper' pipe smokers turned to me during tea-break and said in his rich Dublin accent, 'Son, what the hell is that you're smoking in that bloody toy pipe of yours?' I showed him the packet. He sniffed it and handed it back to me. 'Well, I hope the makers never come near you at rehearsals,' he muttered, 'they'd have you barred'; then later he suggested that maybe he should join me on a visit to the tobacconist's, find me a decent pipe and help me enjoy it a bit more.

Jimmy taught me not to inhale the smoke, but just enjoy the aroma, and maybe that's why I've never been addicted in any way. I have gone for weeks, months and even years without smoking at all and still smoke very little today, but I do enjoy its company.

My next summer show was to be at probably the best known resort for seaside entertainment, Blackpool. It boasted in those days some six or seven major venues, all of which presented seasonal productions featuring big name entertainers. My professional home for the summer months, where I shared honours with comedian Charlie Chester, was to be the Queen's Theatre, previously known as Feldman's, and a place long associated with one of the great names in show business in the north, Jimmy Brennan. For as long as I could remember, his reputation and that of this grand old theatre went hand in hand. Stories about Jimmy were part of backstage gossip right up to the time of his death. Here's one of my favourites, which as the years go by and one witnesses the ups and downs of entertaining, seems like a little lesson in common sense.

I was to learn, as good fortune began to shine a little brighter, that there seems to exist a kind of unwritten law that bad news is best kept from the star. It's considered wiser, I suppose, not to worry him needlessly, he's probably got enough problems just trying to be a star week in, week out. For example, when we mess something up during a recording session, or in the television studio, some thoughtful production assistant will tactfully tell the audience that there's been a little technical trouble. Some promoters are known to be careful not to book supporting acts who might get too much applause and put the star's nose out of joint. But the best example as far as I am concerned has always been related to the star's responsibility for activity at the box office. Over the years I've heard one excuse after another, each one more unlikely than the last:

'Monday has always been a bad day here.'
'It's not you, it was even worse for so-and-so last week.'
'You do know that there's a cup match on here tonight.'
'The boarding house serves dinner at this time you know.'

When business is good, however, seldom does anybody mention how well you've done in spite of all these problems. The simple fact is that they are being kind and don't want you to worry.

Anyway, the tale goes that on one occasion, Jimmy's summer show was doing disappointingly at the box office. Night after night he'd come in to find the theatre only partly filled. He'd make regular visits to the star's dressing room to cheer the poor fellow up. However, it was the star on this occasion who seemed to find an endless stream of explanations for the unsatisfactory attendances.

'We should use a bit more advertising, you know,' he told his boss. 'I've met several people in the last week or so who were surprised to see me. "Gosh, are you in town this year?" they asked me "We haven't seen any posters about."' The following day his excuse was 'I'm told the roads are flooded outside the town after that terrible rain,' and so it went on night after night.

As the weeks went by and things were not improving, Jimmy wondered if his star attraction was ever going to run out of excuses. Wandering into the back of the stalls one evening he found the place less than half full. He could take it no longer.

Walking in to number one dressing room, he raised his hands in a gesture of despair, at the same time silencing any attempts from the star to go through his routine.

'I know, I know,' Jimmy said with tragedy in his voice. 'I've heard all about it, it's that bloody Catholic procession in Bristol.'

The poor chap sitting there I'm sure had no idea that what he was saying each evening had become so predictable, and indeed so ridiculous. We all fall into the trap of forgetting that the other guy has probably heard it all before. Members of the public, on the other hand, say things to us all the time which are no less predictable, not realising that we've heard them hundreds of times. My dear old friend, the late Arthur Askey, who trod the boards while I was at nursery school, made me aware of it when we first did a season together. 'Watch this fella now,' he'd say as he saw some chap approaching, knowing by the look on his face that he was going to stop and make some remark. 'He's either going to say "Get up off your knees then, Arthur," or "You're even

68

smaller than I thought you were."' He was invariably right.

If, by the way, you'd like to avoid some of the most obvious clichés, let me offer you a few tips. For instance, when people are standing around while a personality is signing autographs, try not to fall into the trap of saying,

'Have you got writer's cramp yet?'

Don't hand him a cheque book and ask him to *sign here*. You'll probably be about the third one to do it that morning.

If someone says to the personality, 'You must get fed up doing this,' don't be tempted to chip in with 'It's when people don't ask him he'll have to worry.'

Watch out also for what is probably the greatest chestnut of all, a phrase which I have heard everywhere from the smallest village in Ireland right across the world to Sydney, Australia. 'If you go well in this town you'll go well anywhere. They're very hard to please, you know.'

My most common one is when people see me at a golf club or in a bar or restaurant and say to their friends in a loud voice, 'Oh, look who it is, Sandra! It's Des O'Connor (or Terry Wogan, or Max Bygraves).'

Sadly, Jimmy Brennan's career had ended prior to my initiation into the Blackpool galaxy of summer stars. His passing, in fact, heralded the gradual decline of the Queen's Theatre, which was soon to disappear altogether from the already diminishing list of British theatres. My competition was formidable, to put it mildly, other names occupying a place of honour outside the opposing establishments including Ken Dodd, Des O'Connor, Kenneth McKellar, Adam Faith, Arthur Haynes, the Bachelors, Eddie Calvert, Arthur Askey and many others far better known than myself. Whatever the merits or otherwise of the season, I had a great time. Lynn and I, together with our young daughter, rented a nice bungalow and settled there for four months. Strangely enough the thing I best remember is the wonderful companionship I enjoyed with all my fellow 'pros' on the golf course at St Anne's Old Links. Day in, day out we'd gather there to compete in the most amazing succession of contests concocted over a drink at the bar:

THE OPERA HOUSE . . . THE QUEEN'S . . . THE NORTH PIER
versus
THE CIRCUS . . . THE A.B.C. . . .THE SOUTH PIER

THE ENGLISH . . . *versus* . . . THE REST OF THE WORLD

THE COMEDIANS . . . *versus* . . . THE SINGERS

Visiting artists who happened to play golf would be roped in for these occasions: Donald Peers, Ted Ray, Griff (of the husband and wife act Micki and Griff), and many more. The hospitality extended to us by that particular golf club and its members is something we will always remember with gratitude. It's a relationship that still flourishes to this day. Such was the fervour with which some of these sporting events were approached that I recall one morning when Arthur Haynes arrived having painted his woods, one red, one white and one blue, leaving us foreigners in no doubt as to the quality of his British patriotism. He was quite amazed to find the Rest of the World unwilling to follow suit.

By the end of the season I'd been booked in advance to go to Great Yarmouth the following year accompanied by Arthur Askey.

My 1966 television series seemed to hit the jackpot

and to round things off my latest single *Elusive Butterfly* was taking me again to that enviable position in the upper reaches of the Top Twenty.

In fact, *Elusive Butterfly* was one of those milestones which caused a certain degree of mixed feelings as far as I was concerned. It was written by a young American named Bob Lind, who recorded it over there. I'm not sure of the story of its success in the States, but can remember how enthusiastic everybody appeared to be about my recording it for the British market. I agreed to do what is known in the trade as a 'cover version'; in other words, a similar recording to be released here at home. What I honestly didn't think would happen was that Bob Lind would come over here and promote his original version in this country. The upshot was that we both finished up on *Top of the Pops* singing almost identical versions of the same song, and standing at No. 4 and No. 5 in the charts. It's something I didn't enjoy, since, after all, he wrote the song and created its popularity, and I never set out to compete against him. When I met him at the television studios he was polite and friendly, although I'm sure he must have felt a certain resentment at having to share his moment of glory with someone else. On the other hand, of course, you could argue that as composer of the song he had the achievement of being in the best sellers twice at one time.

Roughing it in the clubs can be hard and sometimes even demoralising work, and most entertainers naturally look forward to the prospect of being elevated to performing in the more exclusive and prestigious rooms. From time to time I'd read with envy that so-and-so was appearing for a month at the Talk of the Town, or that such-and-such an artist was doing a month's engagement at the Savoy in London. You

Giant acacia

never know if these bookings will come your way, when other budding artists will envy you as they sit in some noisy little dressing room flicking through *The Stage*. Since I am one of the people who eventually saw the other side of the coin, it's interesting to be able to write some home truths about the reality of the situation.

I'm sure that many of my colleagues will agree that the Savoy can be either a pleasure, or one of the most difficult and unrewarding engagements an artist could undertake. I went there at a time when I assumed my television popularity was reaching a kind of peak, in the mid-to-late sixties. I was to appear each evening Monday to Saturday for a month. I booked six of the singers from my show, together with my own group of musicians under the supervision of my musical director. I also invited the Gojos to do the season for good measure. Our programme and its staging were carefully planed and we spent all of the opening day hard at rehearsals. (We did, of course, spend the previous week in a private rehearsal room).

'How long did you intend to do?' the resident manager asked me. Being accustomed to cabaret engagements I had assumed that I'd be called on to do at least forty-five minutes or so.

'Well, I was planning on about three quarters of an hour ... what would you advise?' I said, noticing a slight look of surprise on his face.

'Knowing this room as I do,' he said, looking quite serious, 'I'd say that's a bit long.' He had that 'I'm only telling you this for your own good' tone in his voice. But like the man said, 'he knew the room', so I wasn't going to argue with that, at least until I saw how things went on the opening night. He looked through the running order on his desk. 'I'd settle for thirty minutes, top whack, if I were you.' He put the papers down. 'Come on,' he said, 'I'll show you where you're dressing.'

There was some coffee in my room so we sat down and made the necessary adjustments to my programme. He seemed much happier but I was none the wiser about how it was all going to turn out.

I still had the feeling that half an hour was a bit on the short side, but at the same time I knew that I was best guided by the man who worked in the room fifty-two weeks a year. Running through my mind all the time were the words of comedian Dickie Henderson, who had worked there many times and to whom I had spoken about a week previously.

'Oh, you're doing a month at the Savoy, are you?' he said, 'Have you been there before?'

I told him it was my first time. 'I believe it can be very tough,' I said, hoping he would assure me otherwise, or at least throw some light on the situation.

'Well, let me put it this way,' croaked Dickie, in that much-impersonated voice of his, 'it's different ... you'll never really know what kind of reception you're gonna get from one night to another.' I suggested that this was nothing new in cabaret. 'Yeah, but this place is something else,' Dickie went on. 'There'll be nights when you'll probably wonder what you're doing in the business, but then the next evening you'll come off stage wondering if you're still in the same room. One thing is certain, it'll keep you on your toes, and that's not a bad thing.'

I felt very nervous on the Monday night, and frankly, I thought the audience was a bit on the cool side. Tuesday evening things were much better and we all got quite a reception. Wednesday night was just incredible. The young compère thanked the resident dancing girls for their opening routine, chatted for a few minutes while my group got set up, then with great pomp and ceremony announced me, THE

74

STAR OF THE SHOW. I could hardly believe what followed. I can honestly say it was the only occasion in my career, either before or since, when I walked out on to the stage to a great musical fanfare, and not one single person in the entire room clapped, or indeed showed any interest whatever.

The band swung into bright, happy, opening music while I strode from one side of the raised cabaret stage to the other, going through the motions of acknowledging the welcoming applause, which on this occasion wasn't there. It was the strangest experience, everybody simply getting on with their eating and drinking, here and there the odd face turning in my direction in a kind of vague awareness of my being there. Our thirty minute stint ended on that evening to a rather lukewarm round of applause. Every night from then on I was to stand in the wings awaiting my entrance with bated breath.

My dressing room was, in fact, one of the first floor bedrooms, minus the bed, and each evening I'd be there an hour before show time. I wore some specially designed casual wear, in keeping with my television 'uniform' of the time; the band, singers and dancers were wearing appropriate matching colours. About five or ten minutes before zero hour we'd all congregate in the downstairs corridor adjacent to the backstage entrance, sharing our last minute enthusiasm, or lack of it. As I've said earlier, when you've done as much national television as I'd done by then, you could fall into the trap of assuming that most people would know who you were, at least, and that perhaps you're in that category sometimes referred to as 'household names'.

One evening during our second week we assembled as usual in the backstage passage awaiting a cue to stand by for action, when I noticed a small middle-aged couple in elegant evening wear coming down the corridor in our direction, obviously heading for the dining room. When finally they came into earshot I overheard the following (it will help to imagine this conversation in a sort of *To The Manor Born* accent). . .

LADY: 'Oh God, Henry, don't tell me there's a show going on during dinner, I always find it so irritating.'

GENT: 'Yes, I'm afraid so, darling.'

LADY: 'Oh I don't think I could bear it, couldn't we go and eat somewhere else? You know what happened last time, we left.'

GENT: 'Come on darling, it may not be too bad, in fact, I think it's that chap you sometimes watch on the television.'

LADY: 'Which chap is that? You know I don't like television.'

GENT: 'That chap who sits in the chair, and sings rather quaint little Irish songs.'

LADY: 'Really? Can't place him, but I like him, do I?'

GENT: 'Yes, darling, but I promise, if it's too dreadful we can leave and eat later.'

LADY: 'Oh, very well then.'

They disappeared into the dining room leaving the gang and I lost for words. One of them summed up the situation in a nutshell. 'I hope we don't get many of "her" in tonight.' I often wonder if they stayed the course, as I didn't have many quaint numbers in my programme that evening.

I was to make two return visits to the Savoy as a performer the following years. There were evenings, of course, when roles were reversed and I sat among the patrons enjoying a meal, while watching fellow performers go through the hoop. I couldn't help feeling on those occasions that the majority of the guests would have been just as happy to forego the distractions of the stage show and simply get on with dinner, plus the odd knees-up on the dance floor, between courses.

My mother was holidaying with us during the final week of one of my engagements there, so Lynn thought she'd take her along one evening to watch me work. Mom was about eighty at the time and didn't like to be out too late, so this was one of her rare opportunities to see me in a cabaret setting, the show commencing at about nine o'clock.

Like many elderly people she always insisted that the band was far too loud, and would have been much happier had my entire performance been accompanied by Mary O'Hara on her harp. Knowing that Lynn had secured a ringside table I advised our guitarist, who was standing very close to their table, 'Take it easy tonight, my mother will be right next to your amplifier.'

Everything seemed to be going fine, although I did spot her once or twice as she discreetly placed a hand over her ear. With a certain relief I embarked on a Irish folk song. Bright in tempo but very gentle, it was performed at a virtual whisper to my own guitar accompaniment. I'd completely forgotten, however, that it ended very quietly followed by a short, sharp chord from the band. Mother sipped her Chablis, proudly watching her young lad of forty years, his lyrics awaking all kinds of nostalgic memories in them both. The final stanza tailed away in volume, culminating in a surprise punchline. A short pause followed, while the whole thing sunk in, then came the loud, shock chord from the lads. Mom was just about to put her glass down and applaud when the musical explosion occurred. To tell you that her reaction was dramatic would indeed be an understatement. She literally flung her glass of wine into the air as she leaped from her seat.

'Jesus, Mary and Joseph,' she shouted, 'what was that?'

Still coughing and spluttering on the sip of wine she'd been about to swallow, she picked up her little evening bag, and sloshing the guitar player across the shins she said, 'What do you think you're doing, for God's sake, frightnin' the life out of people?' Well, I did warn him.

Any time I glanced towards their table for the remainder of the evening Lynn was wiping the tears from her eyes. In fact she still laughs about it today.

The idea of presenting cabaret in the main dining room was to end some time later. Who knows, maybe Henry bought the place after seeing my act and put a stop to the whole affair for the sake of his wife's digestion.

At the time of writing I'm in the midst of preparations for a television special which I've been asked to do for the BBC. Among my guests on this occasion is the distinguished flautist James Galway. Jimmy has appeared with me on several previous shows and indeed I've made reciprocal visits to his specials. I believe that this relatively recent innovation of classical musicians and singers appearing on such programmes as mine is a welcome one indeed. It has created an added awareness among the general public as to the outstanding talents of such people. Previously their appearances were limited mainly to classical style programmes which naturally kept them away from many people who would think such productions outside their musical appreciation.

Jimmy himself would, I'm sure, be the first to tell

you that this extension of his professional activities has been beneficial both to his musical versatility, and to his talent as a musician/entertainer.

Back in 1966–67, when my television shows had reached such an unexpected level of public acceptance, John Ammonds was keen to broaden our horizons as far as guests were concerned. We were by now, incidentally, winning a viewing audience of some eighteen and a half million, and when you consider the relatively small number of sets there were in Britain at the time, it must have been thought impressive. I was hardly aware of it myself since I was quite new to the television game and hadn't yet become too aware of the 'ratings battle'. Even today I tend to have a slightly philosophical attitude to that side of things. I simply do the very best I can when putting every show together; then all I can hope for is to hold my own. Whether the ratings turn out good or bad, frankly there's not a lot you can do about it except to change things completely. However, this is a kind of panic measure, in my opinion, and you might be better examining your own personal standing in the popularity stakes.

'How about some classical guitar playing next week?' John Ammonds said to me one morning during a rehearsal break. 'Twould be a lovely change, you know, and anyway the guitar is so popular it would go over very well.' I was delighted with the idea myself and told John so. 'I wonder if we could get John Williams to come along and have a chat about the prospects of a guest spot.' John then asked me to carry on with matters in hand while he went and made a few phone calls.

Next day he reported that he'd been in touch with John Williams and that he seemed very keen on the idea.

'I wonder if you could do something together,' my

producer said, thinking of the entertainment value. 'If we find the right idea, and it's just for fun, then I don't see any reason why it shouldn't work.'

'Let's have a think about it,' I said, 'and maybe by the time John comes in we'll have something to suggest to him.'

One of the numbers in the Top Twenty at that time was a single by the Seekers, called *Morningtown Ride*. 'If you could play the tune,' our musical director Ken Thorne suggested, 'then maybe I could write some nice classical style variations for John, then add a string quartet if it feels right. Leave it to me, I'll write something out.'

John Williams came in a few days later. His chosen solo item posed no problems, so we sat and discussed our little duet. Well, the whole thing worked fine and John went away feeling very happy and leaving us likewise. We'd decided to call our little offering *Variations on a Theme from Morningtown Ride*.

That was the first of many visits which John was to make over the years, and like James Galway he admits that his first excursions into light entertainment, or *variety* as it's often called in the television world, were a turning point in his career, strictly from the point of view of his relationship with the general public. His involvement in recent times with the group Sky is a further indication of his willingness to broaden his horizons. In no way does it detract from his classical work or from his serious study of the guitar. On the contrary, it has only meant that he's reaching a far bigger audience, bringing the great joys to be had through his talents to many more people.

Incidentally, during that first week he appeared with me, back in 1966, John happened to read in the trade press that the show was getting the viewing figures I previously mentioned, of eighteen and a half million. He had been, at that time, travelling through the United States giving guitar recitals at various concert halls, many of them houses in that country's colleges and universities. He came into the studio one morning armed with a quite alarming statistic which he'd worked out over dinner the previous evening.

'You know Val,' he said casually, as we sat tuning up our guitars, 'I've worked it out, that in order to reach the same audience in concert, as I'm about to play for tomorrow, I'd need to do a concert every evening for the next eighty-eight years.'

There's food for thought there, you know. The message in my opinion is loud and clear: *if you're going to put your professional reputation on the line by accepting television, then you'd better be sure you've got it right.*

Whatever else may be said about my efforts on television back in those days, I certainly seemed to be 'getting it right' as far as the public was concerned. My contract was renewed and my professional life was nicely rounded off with the news that the Variety Club of Great Britain had honoured me by selecting my name as BBC Television Personality of the Year. The celebratory lunch and presentations followed a month or two later, giving me the privilege of sharing the top table honours with such established stars as Michael Caine, Anna Neagle, Frankie Howerd, Virginia McKenna and David Frost. Those occasions are made all the more special by the knowledge that your name had been chosen by fellow members of your profession.

Lynn completed the year, as far as our personal life was concerned, by presenting the Doonican family with a brand new baby daughter, Fiona Catherine. Somehow we seemed to have the knack of producing girls, and if you take a look at some of the photos included in this volume, you might agree it was a 'happy knack'.

My standing at the box office was by now beginning to show signs of improvement. I was already signed up to do my own show in Great Yarmouth in the summer of 1967, and was to be joined by Arthur Askey. What a pleasure our partnership turned out to be, not just for that year, but also for 1968 and 1969.

Arthur was a joy to work with and I thank him for all he taught me during our time together. His stage-craft was quite superb, as I'm sure all my colleagues who have shared the stage with him will agree. He gently guided me through some of the subtleties, like *where to stand, when to move, where to look*, and in general *how to behave when sharing the stage with other people*. He certainly knew where the laughs were in a routine and demonstrated the art of how to make the most of them. In spite of all my years in the business I somehow became aware that I had entered a part of the first division where I hadn't played a lot, and I'd found a great coach. It's lovely to look back on those hundreds of evenings when I'd listen to him singing away to himself in the next door dressing room as he prepared for the first house. I remember his neatly laid out dressing table with all his personal bits and pieces. There was always the smell of throat pastilles in his room. One of his little idiosyncrasies was to have with him at all times a tin of Meggazones – he'd cut one into several slices and fifteen minutes or so before curtain-up he'd pop a piece in his mouth. Meggazone fumes will always remind me of singing a duet with Arthur. Five minutes before the overture he'd breeze into my room looking like a little Burton's dummy and bubbling with enthusiasm. 'Come along, son,' he'd say, 'I don't think that poor audience can bear to wait for me any longer.' He really did love his work, and showed it. He was an inspiration to all of us.

I said to somebody shortly after his death that

'Arthur was always a hard act to follow on stage, but for sheer professionalism in his career he was impossible to follow.' I'm so glad I knew him.

We were at the Wellington Pier for our season at Great Yarmouth. The business turned out to be quite amazing. We both stayed at the Carlton Hotel just across the road from the pier, our rooms looking out on to the seafront. As the weeks went by we fell into a kind of ritual which we carried out like a couple of overgrown schoolboys who had just come into the business. Each day, if we weren't out playing golf, we'd have a beady eye on the front of the house across the road watching the crowds standing in line to get their tickets for that evening's shows. Time after time we'd spot one of the box-office staff emerge into the sunlight carrying that coveted piece of theatre equipment, the 'house full' sign. Whoever spotted it first would dash to the phone and ring the other, when we'd both chant in unison 'We've done it again, playmate!'

Our opposition in town was again very impressive: Morecambe and Wise, Mike and Bernie Winters, Mike Yarwood, Rolf Harris, Ruby Murray and a host of others. Arthur's show business anecdotes were inexhaustible. I was to learn virtually every word ever uttered by the legendary Eddie Gray of the Crazy Gang. Arthur idolised Eddie's humour and said on many occasions that he thought him to be the funniest man he'd ever met. I feel it is a great shame that Arthur never got around to writing a book about his old friend. I feel sure it would have been quite a classic, and a valuable record of two great comics.

Playing to packed houses was a new experience for me. The only times I'd known it previously was when somebody else was Top of the Bill. My name was now up there and it felt good. In fact, 'being good box office' is one department of the popularity stakes which has always been a bit of a mystery. Some people seem to draw the crowds pretty consistently year in, year out whilst others who appear to be just as popular can't do it. Everybody, of course, however good, blows hot and cold as the years go by, but as with making hit records, you never know for sure if you can make it work again next time around. That's why this is such a great business: no matter how long you're doing it you never cease to feel that old choke chain.

By now, I was taking my own backing group wherever I went, its modest complement forming the bulk of my entourage. They were, of course, part of my show at Yarmouth, eliminating all extra rehearsals with the pit orchestra, so much part of my life until that time. Having your own group of backing musicians, with all its inherent problems, is truly one of the most comforting of perks enjoyed by the more successful entertainers. When the pressure of other commitments makes it difficult for you to attend rehearsals, you really have no need to worry, secure in the knowledge that, should you not turn up until just before show time, the lads will know your every requirement.

Long summer seasons, sometimes extending to four months, can, however, bring their own problems as far as the individual members of your company are concerned. Their personal domestic situations can make it extremely difficult, especially if a young family is involved. They may also have other business commitments needing their attention; they're unavailable for other work, such as recording sessions and broadcasting work, and this can damage future prospects. For all or some of those reasons a change of keyboard player was required before our Yarmouth season. The replacement, a young bearded lad in his mid-twenties, arrived for our first rehearsing session. Neither of us could possibly have conceived what a permanent fixture he was to become in my working life. For nigh on twenty years now, Roger Richards has been the mainstay of my musical support, having taken over as Musical Director in 1969. Over that period, I can honestly say that I've never appeared professionally in a musical capacity without Roger's invaluable support. It's hard to believe, in fact, that since that first rehearsal at Great Yarmouth he has never missed or cancelled a performance for any reason, in spite of all the colds, flu, tummy bugs and other ailments he has chosen to overlook in the line of duty. Looking back, it's even harder to believe that in all that time there's never been a cross word or any hard feelings between us. His contribution to my career has been truly enormous, and invaluable.

Looking into my diary for the autumn of 1967 was quite daunting. Apart from the television series, now very much in the ascendancy, there was the exciting prospect of appearing in my very first Royal Performance. My latest single, *If the Whole World Stopped Lovin'*, was destined to take its place among the top five hit records, and then, of course, there were many lucrative club dates on offer.

This was a period when the theatre clubs around the country reached a quite phenomenal degree of popularity which was to last for years. Large fees were available to the more popular stars of the television and record industry if they were versatile enough to perform effectively in cabaret. Some of these establishments were very large, catering for some fifteen hundred or more people each evening. Dinner or light meals were served at some, while others were nothing more than huge drinking clubs. In an effort to justify the hefty salaries paid for the entertainment, some of the smaller ones crammed so many people in as to make it almost impossible for anybody to enjoy themselves.

I remember an occasion when there really wasn't room for the band and myself on the minute stage or bandstand. If one of us so much as moved to adjust the amplifier controls, it invariably meant knocking over a music stand, and the subsequent chaos trying to retrieve the scattered contents. Roger, facing the stage, his back to the audience, was perched precariously on his adjustable piano stool, inches from the edge of our raised podium. On three sides of us people were packed like sardines around the scattered tables, the men in shirt sleeves, their ladies fanning themselves with anything to hand.

Nevertheless, the show was a resounding success, the audience enjoying themselves, their reaction everything we could wish for in the circumstances. As we neared the end of our allotted time, I noticed a very fat man laboriously make his way between the tables and head in my direction.

'Scuse me Val,' he puffed. 'Will you do me a favour, mate?' I leaned forward, trying not to fall off my bit of the stage. 'My wife Doreen would love you to sing that song *Scarlet Ribbons* – it's her favourite.' I honestly didn't feel the occasion was just right for that particular song, but after what the poor chap had gone through getting to the stage, what could I do?

I signalled to Roger, who nodded his approval and began the gentle introduction, music-box style, high up on the piano. A hush came over the room as I quietly dedicated the song to Doreen. After a gentle ripple of applause, you could have heard the proverbial pin drop, so I began. All went well for the first verse, which ends with a kind of rallentando, or slowing down. At that vital stage the tinkling piano suddenly stopped, its music-box effect replaced for a second or two by a dull thud, then the whole place burst into raucous laughter. 'What the hell is going on?' I thought, looking over my right shoulder in the direction of the silent piano. Roger's head and shoulders had completely vanished from behind the keyboard, but were quite remarkably replaced by his feet, waving about in the air like some strange antennae. The room by now was in uproar, and I stood dumbstruck centre stage. Then, quick as a wink, the legs were gone. Seconds later a red-faced musical director, hair standing on end, came slowly clambering back to his original position.

It appears that Roger's amazing multi-purpose collapsible stool had done precisely that: it collapsed. He went into a kind of Fosbury flop off the stage, landing flat on his back in the middle of an adjacent table, his long legs flailing about overhead. Well, you try following that with the second verse of *Scarlet Ribbons*. Even Doreen had had enough by now.

Like the seasoned campaigners we're supposed to be on such occasions we simply made the most of it, Roger taking bow after bow and yours truly promptly getting into our final routine.

The chap who ran the place thought the whole show was wonderful, and kindly invited us to his private office for a drink. Believe it or not, he later whispered to Roger, 'Damn good entertainer, this man, isn't he? Knows how to keep the audience happy – although I'll be honest, I don't think he needs the gimmicks, like your somersault off the piano stool. Out of character, I thought.'

Roger has never done it since. Shame really!

I shouldn't knock the fact that there were so many people in the club that evening. Overcrowded though it was, I'd choose it anytime in preference to performing before empty tables and chairs. There really can't be anybody in our profession, however pampered by the trappings of stardom, who can honestly deny having suffered those occasions when, for one reason or another, the public didn't turn up.

Back in my radio days I was engaged to appear for one week at a restaurant down in Plymouth. The place itself was nice enough, but unfortunately the public weren't interested in going there. I turned up one evening, only to be told that not a single customer had booked for dinner. The manager, the resident quartet and myself sat and tried to use up some of the coffee they had made, while licking our respective wounds. Assuming the evening was a lost cause, I rose and slipped on my overcoat, ready to enjoy my freedom. Just as I approached the door, it opened, and in walked a family of four, mother, father, daughter and son-in-law. I looked back towards the manager as if to say, 'Surely you don't expect me to...' He looked at me in turn as if to reply, 'It's not my fault, mate,' then he ushered the rather self-conscious foursome to the best table.

Fifteen minutes later the musicians played a half-hearted fanfare, and on came the 'star of the show'. I must have looked pathetic – I certainly felt it. Finishing my opening song, I bowed in the direction of my audience of four, then to my great surprise the head of the family rose to his feet and waved in my direction. 'Why don't you bring your guitar and stool over and join us in a glass of wine?' What a relief.

The following encounter couldn't have been more unexpected. It seems that Mum loved my morning radio show and had specifically requested a visit to the restaurant to see me work. So I sat on my stool, guitar in hand, and without the aid of a microphone sang all the songs she wanted to hear. The band, feeling redundant, retired to the bar, while I stayed with the family for an hour or more.

My first professional gig
– Ireland, mid 40s

The Four Ramblers in
the 50s

My first Music Hall date in England
– early 50s

Summer season with the Four Ramblers at the Gaiety Theatre,
Ayr, Scotland, 1955

'Let's check Fiona's toes,' says
Sarah

Sarah and Fiona pose for photographers

Arthur Askey, Moira Anderson and all the summer cast at Blackpool, 1969

Dear Arthur's OBE celebration at the Opera House, Blackpool, 1969

Cilla and me back in the 60s

Yes, I'm afraid it is Dave Allen. Doesn't he look happy?

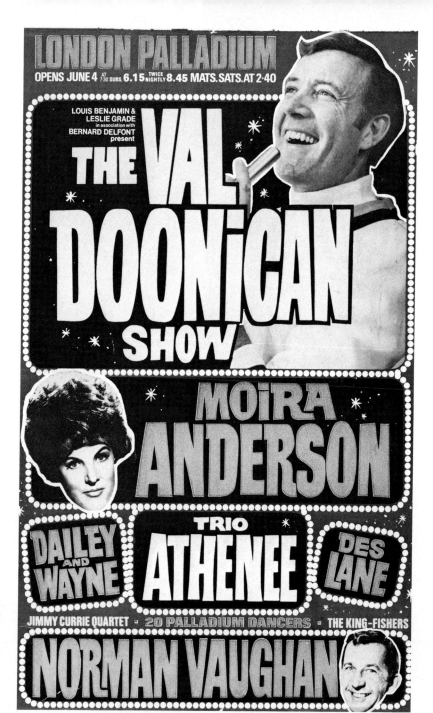

A six month run at the Palladium, 1970

Me, the Irishman; Dickie Henderson, the Englishman;
John Laurie, the Scotsman

Dickie and myself having a flashy shirt competition

With Mary O'Hara. You've guessed it, we were singing an Irish song

Singing a duet with Rosemary Clooney is always a joy

Well, it had to go in somewhere

If you happen to have a well-known face through television or films it's quite common for people to inform you that somewhere in their private world you've got a 'double'. I've heard it happen so many times through the years, but on the few occasions when I've come face to face with the evidence I've been quite puzzled as to why anybody should see a resemblance. One particular occasion that comes to mind was when a Sunday newspaper contacted my manager, telling her of some chap who had come to their attention.

'They say that the man has come into their office, and that the resemblance is quite uncanny,' Eve told me over the phone. 'What they'd love to do is get the two of you together for a photograph for next Sunday's edition.'

Anyway, I agreed to meet them at a London hotel. When I got there they eagerly welcomed me and took me to a private room where their photographer was waiting. A few minutes later my 'double' arrived and we shook hands. I was convinced, once and for all, on that meeting, that you most certainly never see yourself as others do. The man looked a bit like me, I suppose, but what all the fuss was about I just couldn't understand. When the paper came out that weekend everybody I spoke to was as surprised as I was at what little similarity there was. However, the whole thing gave me an idea for my show.

One Saturday night during the series I talked about this whole business of 'doubles', and was fortunate enough to get a few good examples on photographs. Putting the pictures away I then said quite seriously, 'Now the reason I've brought this up tonight is that very recently I did see something that quite stunned me, so much so, that I thought somebody was playing a joke on me. Now I won't tell you too much about it, I'll simply introduce a special guest and leave you to judge for yourselves.' The lights went very low on the set and the spotlights were trained on the stage entrance at the side. There was a rather dramatic roll on the drums and I announced, 'Ladies and gentlemen, from Sevenoaks in Kent, may I introduce Mr Martin Harris.' The audience, filled with anticipation, were on the edge of their seats as they waited. Then, rather nervously, into the spotlight walked Dave Allen. His hairstyle had been completely changed for the occasion, and he wore a heavy sports jacket and corduroy trousers. There were a few seconds of shocked silence, followed by wild applause mingled with Ooohs and Aaahs of approval. 'Good evening, Martin,' I greeted him, 'and thank you very much for joining us tonight.'

He shook my hand and nodded in a kind of shy acknowledgment. 'Hello, Val,' he said quietly in a very well disguised accent, and sounding very 'county'.

After one or two questions and answers, however, we couldn't kid the audience anymore. They began to jeer and giggle, and pretty soon Dave and myself could keep it up no longer and joined in the laughter.

Some five or six years later I was checking into a hotel in Hong Kong. The young Chinese girl behind the reception counter looked up. 'Hello, Mr Doonican,' she said smiling. 'Welcome to Hong Kong. We're enjoying your shows at the moment.' She told me that a series was currently being transmitted on Tuesday nights. I checked into my room and my travelling manager, Mickey, and myself sat down to a cup of coffee. I noticed a copy of the Hong Kong *Television Times* on top of the set in my room and flicked through it. I looked at Tuesday night and there, as the girl had said, was my show. The whole thing was written in the local language, of course, with the 'English subtitles' underneath. I wondered how old the shows were, and thought I might be able to tell by the guest list, so I read. . . 'THE VAL DOONICAN SHOW, with special guests the Smothers Brothers, the Edwin Hawkins Singers, and *Martin Harris*.'

'Who the hell is Martin Harris?' I said out loud; then turning to Mickey, 'Have you ever heard of Martin Harris?'

Mickey looked up. 'Martin who?' he said with a shake of his head. The problem went unsolved for the moment at least. The next day we flew to New Zealand. Halfway through one of the countless meals, Mickey leaned over and gently tapped the back of my hand with the handle of his knife. 'Martin Harris was Dave Allen's double.'

'Brilliant,' I said, 'have a glass of champagne on me.' I'm no fool – Mickey is teetotal, and besides the drinks were on the house, or should I say 'on the plane'.

Casuarina

—— Chapter Four ——

As with my case of mistaken identity, or should I say unmistaken identity at that tobacconist's on the A40, it's good for all of us in the public eye to find ourselves, from time to time, with egg on our faces. I recall one rather special occasion when I really got a plateful.

A very posh luncheon party was laid on by the ATV company at a time when they boasted a formidable stable of successful television stars. The function in question had been arranged so that some special accolades could be awarded to a chosen few. The famous faces making up the guest list were so impressive that the old cliché 'anybody who was anybody' just about fits the bill. I might, for the purpose of my story, inform the reader that Val Doonican was one of the lesser lights and not in line for any of the credits.

A very distinguished gentleman in a dark suit, sporting a red carnation in his buttonhole, made the closing speech and sat down to warm applause. He had mentioned in passing that he had a further appointment and asked us to forgive him if he slipped away once his duties had been performed. In fact, as we got back to our conversation, coffee and cigars, he quietly left the top table and began to shuffle his way between the others, nodding farewells to those who caught his eye. He paused at our table and said hello and goodbye, then to everybody's surprise he turned in my direction and extended an open hand.

'May I just say a special hello to you, old boy,' he said beaming. All eyes were on me as I stood up to take his hand. 'You've been a great favourite with my family,' he kindly told me. 'So may I thank you for all the pleasure you've brought us.'

'Thank you for saying so,' I said, 'I'm flattered.' I prepared to sit down, but he turned to all my famous colleagues.

'My dear mother thinks this man is the cat's whiskers,' he told them, 'and it's not just a passing fancy, she's followed his career right from the start when he had his first records like *My Old Man's a Dustman*.'

He waved goodbye as I slowly slumped into my chair. 'Congratulations, Lonnie,' somebody said. Well, you have to laugh like everybody else!

My summer season for 1969 was in Blackpool. It was nice to be back there after three years, especially since I was starring, not at one of the smaller theatres as previously, but at the prestigious No. 1 venue, the Opera House. The show was to run twice nightly Monday through Saturday from mid-June right through till early October, when the illuminations were finally switched off.

Arthur Askey, once again, occupied the dressing room next to mine, while the lovely Moira Anderson joined as the show's leading lady. The bill also included a dynamic vocal and instrumental group from

Greece, the Trio Athene, and the indispensable Des Lane.

The staging by Ross Taylor was truly lavish, by any standards, and I'm glad to say the business throughout more than lived up to expectations.

The family and I took up residence for that summer in a house at Lytham St Anne's, a few blocks from the famous champion golf course of the same name. As luck would have it, Royal Lytham Golf Club were hosts to the British Open Championship that same year, an unexpected perk for the golf enthusiasts among the visiting entertainers. Practically all of the other Blackpool courses were reserved during the previous week to enable the hundreds of hopefuls not fortunate enough to gain automatic entry to the championship proper to get through the pre-qualifying rounds. This gave many of us the opportunity of visiting the 'tented village' at Royal Lytham, and of watching the 'big boys' at practice. We were not to know at that time, of course, that this was to become one of the most exciting British Opens of all time from a British point of view. Having feasted on the action all week, both on the course and in the comfort of our sitting rooms, we had to content ourselves with savouring those final breathtaking moments on Saturday evening from our theatre dressing rooms, just around show time. It was unforgettable to hear Henry Longhurst describe the historic closing scenes as Tony Jacklin brought the ultimate golfing accolade back to Britain after so many years. Playing that great course over the following months was to take on a new meaning for all of us golfing fanatics.

Another 'veteran' of the Music Hall was in Blackpool at the same time as Arthur Askey and myself: his name was Billy Tasker. A delightful gentleman he was, with an impish personality. He and Arthur were

95

old pals and spent quite a bit of time together on the golf course. They didn't consider themselves to have the same staying power as the young bloods and were more inclined to slip away for nine holes or so when the coast was clear. On occasions, however, we did join forces and it was great fun. If a fairly good player went off the tee and smashed a long drive down the fairway, they'd look at each other and plan their strategy.

'Now, my old friend,' Billy would say to Arthur, 'do you think you can outdrive him? I know I can if I really want to, it's just you I'm worried about.'

Arthur would size up the situation, tee up his ball, then winking at Billy would say, 'Tell you what, I think I'll hit a bad drive on this hole [which was more than likely] 'cause I've got a terrific idea for my second.'

It was such a joy playing with fellows who didn't get too serious about it, which so many of us did, probably spoiling the fun for others. I played quite a bit with two lads who really drove other golfers mad. They argued all the time over little things like the giving of short putts, or whether one moved while the other was playing, causing him to slice or hook. Things got so bad one afternoon, that having had a five minute slanging match on the tee, one of them slammed his driver back into his golf bag, and threw it over his shoulder.

'I'm sick and tired of playing with you,' he stormed. 'It's one . . .ing thing after another, this game is supposed to be for . . .ing pleasure, so play on your own, I'm . . .ing off.' And so he did. All alone he marched off the tee and headed for the club house, about a mile across the course. We stood and gaped for a minute.

'What do we do now?' I asked. 'We've played twelve holes, the match is all square, and you've got no partner.'

'Oh bugger him,' said the wounded one, 'let him go, we'll play on and start a new game with three of us.' He teed up his ball. . .' Anyway, he won't be able to open the car, I've got the keys, so let him wait for a lift home.'

With all the resentment and frustration accumulated over the previous few minutes transmitting itself to the golf club, he walloped the ball. It veered off to the right, going like a rocket. To our horror, we watched the white dot flying, as if guided by some kind of homing device, in the direction of his homeward bound partner. 'Fore,' we shouted in unison, but our sulking primadonna refused to budge. Our second chorus was too late. The ball smacked him on the back of the neck, and we saw him stumble under the weight of his clubs, falling forward on to his knees as if he had just been shot by John Wayne. 'Jesus,' we shouted this time and, as if released by a starting pistol, set off at a sprint in his direction.

He was scrambling to his feet when we got there, and positively seething with rage. He pushed us aside.

'Clear off and leave me alone,' he bellowed, 'Don't touch me.' The final bit sounded like a line Elizabeth Taylor would come out with when her drunken lover tried to apologise. He flung his golf bag over his back, almost spinning himself out of control. Then came a classic line that I shall never forget. Turning to his guilty-looking partner he yelled, 'You! You did that on purpose, you rotten bastard.'

Now, I ask you, especially if you've ever tried to play this impossible game of golf, to consider the probability of such a thing. His partner, like most of us, found it difficult enough to hit the fairway, or a green fifty foot wide, but hitting a fellow's neck from about a hundred and thirty yards? Well, that could certainly be called Target Golf. However, they were

97

back playing together a few days later, arguing as before, each one completely sure that it was the other fellow who caused all the bother.

It takes a lot to deter golfers; they play with back-ache, toothache, colds, coughs or anything else. They play in flaming hot sunshine, freezing cold weather, rain, hail and snow, always somehow convinced it will all change for the better any minute.

I played with some friends of mine in thick fog one morning. The whole thing was quite ridiculous on reflection. We could barely see the end of the teeing area, and there we were slamming the balls into oblivion, then setting out like a search party in the hope of finding them, only to repeat the exercise ad infinitum. When we eventually found our way to the clubhouse bar, one member of our expedition related a great story. We were, at the time, touring on the music halls and were all 'pros'.

It was on just such a foggy morning that he and three fellow members of the cast made their way to a local course, convinced that the fog would soon lift. There wasn't a soul about the place as they enquired about paying green fees.

Entering the club house, they found a lone member of the bar staff cleaning some glasses while a cleaning lady started her chores in the men's lounge.

'You're not going out in that, are you?' the barman jeered.

Rather embarrassed, one of the lads replied, 'Ah well, it might not be too bad, once we're out there. Can we pay some green fees?'

'You pay them at the pro's shop,' the barman told them, 'but he's not in yet, he's not as daft as you lot.'

The lads awkwardly stood about looking at such interesting things as photographs of past captains and presidents adorning the walls. They didn't like to ask for coffee – somehow the conditions weren't right. The barman, carrying a large tray of clean glasses, walked across the lounge. As he reached the door he paused, 'If you want to go ahead, gents, you can pay the green fees when you get back, that's if you ever do get back.'

The four said thanks and went in search of the changing rooms. The fog seemed even more dense when they reached the first tee, and they were relieved at not being visible from the clubhouse windows, just behind them. The first man to go off the tee stood there as if blindfolded, wondering just where the hell the fairway was situated. 'Here goes lads,' he sighed, as if going off the high diving board for the first time. He didn't have the cheek to say 'Keep your eyes on this for me', as golfers often do. 'Crack', went the drive. They all gazed into the fog, but not for long. The sound of the club against the ball was almost immediately followed by the sound of shattering glass, coming from the direction of the clubhouse. The culprit stood dumbstruck, and then slowly turned to his friends.

'What the hell was that?' he said.

One of them almost whispered, 'How could the ball get back there?'

The driver shrugged his shoulders in disbelief. 'Did, did I do that?' then, endeavouring to look even more invisible than they already were, they picked up their bags and slunk into the gloom.

You can just imagine the conversation that took place on their way around the course. 'Well, let's just say it certainly wasn't us. They can't prove anything, can they?'

'Who else could it be, there wasn't another golfer 'round the place for miles.'

'How about saying we found our ball up the fairway? It couldn't be us.'

99

'Suppose the ball finished up in the men's lounge – what then?'

'Let's just get in the car and slip away.'

'No, they know we're at the theatre, they'd have us for not paying green fees as well.'

'Surely they must be insured against things like that. Do you think so?'

'What? Insurance wouldn't cover four lunatics playing in thick fog.'

One thing is certain, not much concentration was given to playing golf over the next few hours. By the time they had made their perilous journey down the eighteenth fairway, the fog had completely gone, and they were able to see the club house quite clearly. Any moment, they expected to see the daunting figure of the secretary in blazer and grey slacks approach them, but no. In fact, it wasn't until they walked off the final green that they came face to face with the result of the early morning's disaster. A large sheet of some kind of transparent paper had been fixed temporarily over a huge gaping hole in the plate glass window of the main lounge. 'It wasn't a dream,' they thought. 'What now?' They changed their shoes, donned their jackets and ties, took a deep breath and headed for the bar. One or two members were sitting chatting over some drinks. The barman was the first to speak. 'Ah, the men of the moment. Your ears must have been burning this morning. The lads couldn't believe anybody could play in that weather. You deserve a drink.'

That wasn't a bad start, anyway. They graciously accepted the offer, and sat chatting with the members, and their new-found friend the barman.

'Actually it was very enjoyable after the first few holes, we had quite a laugh,' one of them lied. Then he bought everybody a drink.

'We didn't have a laugh when you went off the tee,' the barman said. 'Didn't you hear that window go?'

As one voice, and looking as harmless as four altar boys, they chanted, 'Window, which window? What happened?' while at the same time looking at every window in the room except the right one.

'The plate glass, down there,' the barman pointed. 'I'm amazed you didn't hear the almighty crash it made.'

'Goodness me,' one of the lads gasped, 'how the hell did that happen?'

'This is it,' the others thought, 'how much money do we have on us?'

'Poor old Flo, the cleaner,' the barman said, shaking his head and pouring a pint. 'Got the flex of the damned Hoover caught up under a stack of chairs, tipped them over and bang, right through the window. She was so shaken up, bless her, that we had to let her go home.'

The four lads swapped glances, not daring to smile. 'Poor Flo,' they thought, 'maybe we should have a whip-round.' But they left well enough alone, said their goodbyes and thank yous and sought out the pro's shop.

'Are you the fellows who played in the fog?' he asked as he opened the green fee book. 'You deserve some sort of medal.' They felt as though they'd earned one.

Various representatives from the Bernard Delfont office in London (who were responsible for promoting the show in Blackpool) paid us regular visits, each of them leaving us in no doubt that everybody was very happy with the results. One such visitor was Leslie McDonnell, the managing director of Moss Empires Ltd. He watched the show, after which he took Arthur, Moira and myself out for a late-night meal at a local hotel restaurant, which was very popular with the show business fraternity. His enthusiasm for our performances, plus the subsequent results at the box office, was evident from the start, and we spoke of very little else while we enjoyed our meal. The main reason, however, for his visit was to confirm, what up to then had been merely an idea, that the show 'en bloc' should open the following summer for a six-month run at the London Palladium. One small problem remained, however. Arthur Askey was booked to appear there for the forthcoming 1969 pantomime season, and it was felt, understandably enough, that he couldn't very well follow one season at this world famous theatre with another. A replacement had to be found. Meanwhile, my sights were set on more immediate commitments, namely my 1969 television series.

By now, my producer, John Ammonds felt that maybe it was time to move on to something different, so it was mutually agreed that the reins should be handed over to a young producer who had, in fact, worked for a while as John's assistant. His name was Terry Hughes. Terry (now working very successfully in Hollywood) worked on the show for two years, before going on to create many BBC hit shows, not least *The Two Ronnies*, eventually forsaking his producer/director role to take on the mantle of BBC Head of Light Entertainment.

When the 1970 London Palladium season came around, Arthur's role was very successfully taken over by Norman Vaughan. He and I were to work together quite a lot throughout the show, one very enjoyable duo being a golfing number which I'd written in partnership with the late Ronnie Taylor. It was called *Put Down a Ball, Pick Up a Club, and Swing!* It was along the lines of the classic Crosby song *Straight Down the Middle*, and was to be sung by Norman and me while I shot imitation golf balls out into the auditorium. We set the number up in a way which suggested that the theatre was a golf course, which we were both playing for the first time. The opening hole was straight ahead, the second, a short hole into one of the boxes, while the third was on to an elevated green supposedly up in the circle. The patrons, of course, had no idea what to expect as we smacked the balls in their direction, the result being much audience reaction, which is precisely what we wanted.

On the first night, however, it was the opening duet that stopped the show. Norman, at that time, was very much linked, in the public's mind, with the promotion of Rose's Chocolates, his catch-phrase being 'Rose's grow on you'. This phrase, you may well remember, was accompanied by the spectacle of roses growing all over his jacket, ending with a rose popping out of his hand while he made a thumbs up sign accompanied by his famous 'Ooh'.

The idea was that when I first introduced him, at the top of the show, he was to enter covered in roses. I would then act as though I didn't understand the reason for it, never having seen the TV advert. Then our conversation went:

NORMAN: Oh, come on, you don't mean to say that you've never seen me wear this on TV?

VAL: Never.

NORMAN: Well, ask the audience about my catch-phrase.

VAL: What catch-phrase?

NORMAN: Ask them, if they met me in the street wearing this jacket, what would they say?

VAL: OK. (*To audience*) What would you say if you met Norman wearing this jacket in the street?

NORMAN: (*to audience*) One, two, three!

AUDIENCE: *Rose's GROW on you.*

As so often happens on opening night, things didn't quite work out as planned. Norman entered, rose-covered, to great applause, and everything was fine until:

NORMAN: Ask them, if they met me in the street wearing this jacket, what would they say?

VAL: OK. (*To audience*) What would you say if you met Norman wearing this jacket in the street?

VOICE FROM GALLERY: Piss off, you silly sod!

Well, I don't need to tell you what that did to our opening routine. The audience laughed for a good couple of minutes, leaving Norman and me so hysterical that we found it almost impossible to go on. In the circumstances we decided to rephrase our script slightly to avoid repeating the indignity.

Our little golf routine worked very well indeed and, like the opening spot, brought its share of surprises.

One particular Saturday night we were thoroughly enjoying the reaction of an exceptionally responsive audience, as we cracked the polystyrene golf balls into the darkness of the auditorium. When the time came for me to direct one of my shots at the box situated on the left of the stage, we both looked up to see a group of smiling people leaning over the edge, as if daring me to hit them. Norman shouted 'Fore,' but they persisted, knowing the possibility of my getting the ball anywhere within feet of them was remote. He then moved in their direction and, addressing a bespectacled man in the middle of the group, said, ''Scuse me, sir, but I do hope those are not your best glasses. This man is deadly accurate. I would remove them if I were you.' The gentleman laughed heartily, but removed his glasses nevertheless, as if taking

Norman's advice seriously. One of the spotlights slowly moved to one side, gradually illuminating my target and all went quiet. I took a few preliminary waggles at the ball, then *wham*. To our amazement, and indeed everybody else's, it went like a rocket off the centre of my clubhead, and absolutely dead on line for the box. Our good-natured customer stood his ground, still smiling until a split second later it caught him, exactly where Norman had predicted, on the bridge of his nose. As one, he and his party jumped to their feet and cheered their appreciation. The whole theatre joined in the spontaneous ovation, while I modestly took bow after bow.

When all the excitement had died down, I thought I should apologise to the gentleman, just in case I'd caused him any discomfort. 'Not at all, it's quite all right, old man,' he said. 'Worth it just to see such a wonderful shot. I'm bringing a whole party of friends here next weekend, we'll look forward to seeing you do it again.'

We were doing thirteen shows a week, including three performances on Saturday, which meant spending something in the region of forty hours a week backstage. But we took it all in our stride, as entertainers do, the adrenalin which flowed with the success of the show far outweighing any weariness we may have been feeling. There was also the fact that we were an extremely happy company, everybody looking forward to each performance, and all enjoying each other's company.

A select group of British entertainers were, at that time, making variety shows for the ATV company, run by Sir Lew Grade (now Lord Grade). Notable among them were Tom Jones, Engelbert Humperdinck and Des O'Connor. Then one day, my agent, Eve Taylor, was approached about the prospect of my name being added to that list. We were in no doubt whatever as to the enormity of the decision facing us. On the plus side, I was to be guaranteed a series of thirteen one-hour shows of my own to be transmitted all over America, as well as being sold to most English-speaking countries around the world. It did, however, mean my severing a long-standing and very personal partnership with BBC Television, putting my whole popularity, as far as the British public were concerned, in a pretty vulnerable position. There was no way of knowing how the new mid-Atlantic shows would turn out, of course, and this was at a time when the British viewing public had a certain scepticism about artists leaving the BBC to work on 'the other side', for what they always judged to be monetary reasons. I don't think the suspicion is quite as prevalent today, since it is difficult to keep track of the comings and goings between the four channels. In the sixties, however, you were either with BBC or ITV and somehow, to many people, the two didn't mix.

My own instincts told me to stay where I was, but then, as I have already said, I've never been all that ambitious, but simply happy to enjoy what I'm doing as long as it's working well, and I feel it's as good as I can do. But as far as my overall career was concerned, I was being made an offer which I couldn't and really shouldn't refuse.

Having severed my contractual ties with BBC Television, and facing a kind of interval before tackling the international series, I thought it would be a good idea to flex my muscles, so to speak, in my new environment. Eve arranged with the ATV company that I should make a Christmas special for the commercial channel (my first ever starring TV show that didn't have the BBC name on). I suppose it was only to be expected that everybody concerned would be pulling

Yucca

out all the stops to make it a success – after all I was the much publicised new boy, even to the extent of having my own private parking space, identified by a special name plate, outside the front entrance of the studios – a luxury never extended to me either before or since. (Car parking has now reached such heights of priority, that I've actually heard of executives who are prepared to forego a raise in salary in exchange for the privilege of parking their car without any hassle.) The set for the Christmas special was one of the most impressive and elaborate I've ever known in any show. It was built along the lines of the interior of a rather imposing country mansion. Entrance hallway, library, study, bar, lots of beautiful woodwork and beams, a huge log fire burning in the grate, the whole thing festooned with decorations, including, of course, a magnificent Christmas tree shimmering with lights and baubles. It really was a breathtaking piece of design. My guests included Sandie Shaw, Jimmy Tarbuck, Ronnie Corbett, Henry Cooper, Eamonn Andrews and the late Graham Hill. It was one of those shows that had such genuine atmosphere, that from the very start it was a sure winner. Messrs Tarbuck and Corbett were superb: I can't remember when I've seen the whole cast of a TV programme laugh so spontaneously throughout a show, as on that occasion. One of the sketches included in the show was supposedly happening during a Christmas party. I'd been given a magical crock of gold which, when rubbed in the manner of Aladdin's lamp, would fulfil one's most fantastic wishes.

The action began with Ronnie Corbett wishing that, just for once in his life, he could be a big man. This was followed, with the aid of trick photography, by Ronnie's transformation into Henry Cooper. Next came yours truly, wishing that, instead of being so laid back and slow, I could be the fastest man in the world. Val then becomes Graham Hill. Both Henry and Graham were 'surprise guests'.

The sketch was concluded by my asking Tarbuck what his dearest wish would be. He began to rub the crock of gold, his eyes gazing at me.

'I hope you won't find this embarrassing, Dooners,' he began, 'but all my professional life, I've had a great hero. He's Irish, he's suave, he's handsome, he's got a lovely voice and is everybody's favourite, so just for one moment, please may I be my hero?' His touching speech is followed by the predictable flash and transformation, but to everybody's surprise Jimmy becomes Eamonn Andrews. What we didn't know, however, was that Jimmy had secretly tutored Eamonn in the art of putting his thumb and forefinger of each hand into his waistcoat, à la Tarbuck, and endeavouring to tell a gag in the most dreadful Scouse accent. It was one of the funniest situations I can remember in any show I've done and helped to make my initiation into commercial television a very painless experience.

My opening dialogue made special reference to the set, indicating that it was to be my home for the Christmas holiday. I even went so far as to say, 'Sorry I can't take you up the grand staircase to have a look at the bedrooms. In fact, the other side of that partition is where Tom Jones is rehearsing his show.'

Even after that, in came the letters: 'My goodness, what a lovely home you have, a long way from your little place in Ireland. Thank you for letting us see your home. I live quite near you, and I must say that it looks nothing like that from the outside. What a chore for your dear wife, having all those workmen about the place putting up lights and things. Hope you didn't have to keep making tea and coffee for them.'

The proposed series of shows on the horizon was to

be bought and screened by ABC Television in America, as well as being transmitted at home by ATV. A London-based representative of the American company was pretty familiar with what the *Val Doonican Shows* were all about and must have been impressed enough for the deal to have gone so far towards finalisation. Word got through to me, however, that a further entourage were coming in from the States to see me work.

Naturally, my being at the London Palladium was about as good a shop window as anybody could want, and put me at a distinct advantage. Working at the world's leading variety theatre, in what was by now a well-established stage show, doing what I did best, was as much as I could hope for. Well, to paraphrase an old saying, they came, they saw, they contracted, the result being an invitation from Sir Lew Grade to Eve and me, asking us to come to his office for the signing of the agreement.

Once again, the whole deal was splashed all over the newspapers, the accent, of course, being on the amount of money I was allegedly being paid. Headlines announced VAL SIGNS ON DOTTED LINE FOR FIVE MILLION POUNDS. The five million figure was a hypocritical lie, I'm afraid. If the show ran five years, and was sold to all the potential markets open to such marketing, then maybe it could eventually reach something in that region. That, however, is not in any way meant to undervalue the whole thing, it was a dream come true for any television performer such as myself, hosting his own show. So we signed up and kept our fingers crossed.

A producer and director were flown in from Hollywood and two American writers were contracted, while on our side, we had a co–producer and writer keeping an eye on the British side of things. One of the ingredients vital to the show, according to the

American team, was some British comedy, preferably something which could be resident, as it were, throughout the series. Great interest was focused on a comedy series running on ATV at the time, starring that very talented comedy actor Bernard Cribbins, assisted by the equally gifted Sheila Steafel and Bob Todd. It was decided that their contribution would be based in a London pub called the Flying Ducks.

It was virtually impossible to chose a weekly array of guests which would have equal appeal on both sides of the Atlantic, but we all worked very hard on the shows, and I must say, no expense was spared.

When finally we had thirteen hours of material 'in the can', I was asked to travel to the United States for a promotional trip. Eve, Lynn and I flew to New York, where we were booked in at the St Regis Hotel. During the following ten days or so, I was to be faced with an exhausting succession of radio and television appearances, coupled with endless newspaper interviews and photographic sessions, in an intensive effort to promote my name to a brand new audience.

In fact, the only familiar face I was to see throughout was that of David Frost. His very highly rated talk show was running at the time, and he spared no effort to make my appearance an enjoyable and indeed an effective one. Then there was the Dick Cavett show, the Mike Douglas show in Philadelphia, and many more.

My sister Nancy emigrated to America as a GI bride way back in my youth. Since she lived in Philadelphia, she and her family were in the audience as I appeared on the highly successful *Mike Douglas Show*, and for me it was a memorable experience. She had, in fact, never seen me work before, even though she had naturally followed my career with great pride. After the show we had a meal together and talked endlessly of our respective lives since our last meeting. Lynn and I stayed on in New York for a few days and managed to see a few Broadway shows. All in all we had a wonderful time and both felt that come what may, the experience was something we wouldn't have missed.

I found the American journalists more inclined to enquire about early life in Ireland, and the years leading to my initial steps into the entertainment world, than any of my more recent achievements. In spite of the obvious cynicism which seems part and parcel of that profession, especially amongst its more seasoned campaigners, I found them at times genuinely amused and even moved by my stories of my early childhood. As a result, I began recalling and rekindling all manner of riches which until then had lain dormant somewhere in my memory.

One particular lady from a New York paper was, in fact, so fascinated by what life was like for a young Irish lad in those far off days, that our luncheon appointment stretched far beyond its allocated time. As we finally prepared to vacate the already deserted restaurant, she gathered up her scattered belongings.

'Tell me something,' she said, 'have you ever thought of writing down all that stuff you've been telling me?' My reply was in the negative, to which she simply muttered 'Pity!' When we got to the door we shook hands. 'Thanks again,' she said, 'and try to do something about writing your stories: show business is so full of hyped up rubbish that it's nice to hear some genuine stuff. Don't set out to write a book, just write it down as it was, and if there's a book there, all the better. Chances are, it'll be a good one.'

We parted, never to meet again, but her advice stayed with me, although it was many years afterwards that I bought the first writing pad.

It was also around that time that Lynn and I were invited to spend a short holiday in the South of France, with film director Ken Annakin and his wife Pauline, friends of ours who had a beautiful home in the mountains overlooking Cannes. The evening after our arrival, our hosts arranged for us to join them for dinner at the house of some film colleagues.

Pulling up outside a delightful waterside villa at Cap Ferrat we were both delighted and surprised to be warmly greeted by none other than David Niven and his lovely wife Hjordis. A quite memorable evening was to follow, as David, a most charming and entertaining man, kept us enthralled with reminiscences of life in the movies. In fact, all of us, inspired by his well-known skills as a raconteur, chatted on into the small hours, recalling stories from our respective childhoods. When finally we stood making our farewells, David shook my hand and said, 'You write those stories down, old boy, if only to pass on to your grandchildren. Otherwise they'll be gone forever, and that would be a shame.'

I waited with bated breath for the reaction on both sides of the Atlantic when screening time came around.

There is no doubt in my mind that the folks back home didn't like the shows, for the simple reason that they weren't the same as they'd always been. The sketches and lavish production somehow disarmed people who had become so accustomed to my many series from the BBC Television Theatre. I actually had many letters from 'dyed in the wool' BBC viewers who watched, simply to see what I was up to 'on the other side' as they put it. The letters said, 'We think you have spoiled the shows, and don't think we'll be watching again, but good luck anyway.'

The reaction in the States was mixed, my reviews ranging from very enthusiastic to indifferent.

Remarkably, several reviewers came to the same conclusion as I did myself, that the shows somehow did not seem to match my own television personality as my previous ones had done. The American producers and directors had not seen me work prior to their arrival in London, and simply built a show around me from their experience of working with other people, not through knowing what had made me popular in the first place. It was a shame they didn't know a bit more about my work to start with. But then, that's show business, as they say. By the end of that year and after much soul searching, Eve and I agreed to call it a day and return to making shows for the British market. We will really never know why the thing didn't work better.

Maybe I was just not right for the American TV public. Maybe I was doing the wrong kind of show for them, or, as Jimmy Brennan from the Queen's Theatre in Blackpool would have said, 'Maybe there was a Catholic procession in Buffalo.'

Tucked away in the drawer of my desk at home is an object which serves as a constant reminder of autograph hunters, and one in particular. I have no idea who she is, or where she is, or what she looks like, but she will always remain in my memory.

My manager Eve and I had a battle year after year, arguing about what songs we should release as single recordings. She would choose one and I would shake my head, then I'd suggest a track I'd just recorded and she in turn would 'pooh pooh' the idea as being ridiculous. Well, shortly after I'd had a very big hit with a song called *What Would I Be*, written by singer Jackie Trent, she very excitedly told me of a new song she'd heard. I sat obediently in her office and listened to a demonstration recording of it, and predictably enough, couldn't see anything in it. After endless coaxing and cajoling, Eve could see that I was not going to be convinced. 'Listen,' she said, hand on heart. 'I don't often ask you to do something just for me, but I know I'm right, love. Now, for once take my word and do it.' I surrendered, and promised to include it in a forthcoming recording session.

'It's fabulous,' she shouted on hearing the playback at the recording studio. 'You won't regret it.' A few months later it came out, had every bit of promotion available, and disappeared without a trace. Shortly afterwards a little package arrived at my home. The attached message read: 'From you know-it-all lady manager, sorry, I was wrong, but I still think it was lovely, Love Evie.' Inside was a superb solid gold matching pen and pencil set bearing the simple inscription 'Val'. It really was a lovely thing for her to have done and I was very touched by it. Since I am one of those all time losers as far as personal possessions are concerned – keys, pipes, lighters, glasses, wallets, money clips (and full ones at that) – Lynn absolutely forbade me to take the things out of the box, and there they lay for ages. Then while I was making a special appearance at the Palladium, and having lost my other pens, I took the gold ballpoint from its padded cell and popped it in my pocket.

An enormous crowd awaited the artists outside the stage door after the show, autograph books were being passed from one person to another, and cheap plastic pens, of course, were changing hands. At one point I found myself penless as a nice lady said, 'Please sign this for me, Mr Doonican.' Reaching into my pocket, I produced my solid gold, specially engraved heirloom and wrote my name with a flourish. 'Thank you so much,' she said, smiling as I handed her the book and the pen, as I had been doing to dozens of people previously. Too late I discovered my folly and frantically searched with my eyes through the sea of people in the vague hope of seeing that gentle face. But the lady was nowhere to be seen. I've never forgotten her, though. She took the pen, knowing it was mine. She knew it was a special possession, being solid gold and having my name engraved on it. There is no possible way she could think I handed them out like some sort of souvenir. I'm sure she's still got it and has had fifteen to twenty years in which to feel guilty enough to send it back. Each time I reach into my drawer and produce its lovely bedmate, the propelling pencil, bearing my name, I wonder where it is now. The only excuse I could find in defence of the lady would be if her name was Valerie. That way she could flaunt it about quite unshamedly pretending it was hers.

On one or two occasions when I've been sitting in Eve's office signing papers she's remarked, 'Why don't you use the lovely pen I gave you?'

I've lied through my teeth and said, 'Oh no, I'm keeping that for a very special occasion.' I just couldn't bring myself to tell her I'd been so careless with such a lovely gift.

So after all these years, if that lady is out there with my pen bearing my name, would she please send it back to me, or as a last resort let me have her address so that maybe I could send her the pencil too. At least it would be nice to think of the pen and pencil having a reunion after such a long time.

Many of the guests I had on my ATV series came in from the States, since most of our entertainers, apart from the occasional pop groups, weren't all that successful over there. People like Eddie Albert the actor, Burl Ives, Howard Keel, Jerry Reed the country guitarist, Ray Stevens of *Everything is Beautiful* fame, Petula Clark and many more joined me for the series. Most of them, in fact, were unknown to our daughters who, at that time, were very young and much more impressed by our own internationally or nationally known names ... the Beatles, Basil Brush, the Bay City Rollers and, of course, the stars from *Playschool*.

We sat round the breakfast table one morning prior to my leaving for the studio. I used to drop the girls off at junior school on my way. They were happily munching their Rice Crispies or Shreddies.

'Dad,' said Fiona, speaking with her mouth full. 'Who's on your show this week?' I mentioned somebody. She wasn't impressed. 'Who else?' she asked. I mentioned the remaining guests, finishing with the name Phil Harris. 'Who's he, Dad? Is he a singer?' There was no point in mentioning *Darktown Poker Club* or *Woodman Spare That Tree* to a four year old, so I gave it some thought. Then I had a brainwave.

'You've seen *Jungle Book*?'

'Yes, you took me.'

'Well, you remember Baloo the Bear?'

'Yes, he scratched himself all the time.'

'Well, Baloo the Bear was Phil Harris.'

'Was he really, Dad? Have you got a bear on your show then?'

'Not exactly, but it was Mr Harris who did the voice.' I knew she wouldn't understand. 'Baloo himself was just a cartoon.' That was a bit like saying there was no Santa Claus! I changed the subject, asked her to get ready for school and went to get the car out of the garage. Lynn saw them both into the back seat, and we headed for school. When I dropped them at the gates and was just about to say cheers and be on my way, Fiona handed me a crumpled brown paper bag.

'What's that, darling?' I asked.

'It's for Mr Harris, it's a present.' They ran into school, shouting greetings to their young friends, while I got back in the car. Before pulling away I sneaked a look in the bag – it contained a banana. Phil Harris was tickled pink!

Some years back I told a story concerning Fiona, while appearing on a chat show. She was at a girls' convent at the time. Many years having elapsed since the actual incident occurred, she got quite a ribbing from her young lady classmates, and made me promise I wouldn't repeat the indignity. Now that she's quite a young woman, the worry of embarrassment has subsided and she gives her blessings to the following paragraphs.

The setting, once again, was our breakfast room. The background noise, as before, was the munching of breakfast cereals.

'What will you be doing at school today?' Lynn asked, pouring her a drink.

'Oh, I'm not sure,' she said between slurps, 'probably learning numbers,' slurp, 'singing,' slurp, 'painting, and maybe we'll play *When Suzy was a baby*.'

'What's *When Suzy was a baby*?' Lynn enquired.

'It's a very good game, Mummy, I like it.'

'But how do you play it?' I said.

'Well,' she blurted, settling herself in her chair and rolling her eyes towards heaven, as if asking for guidance. 'Ah . . . it's all about Suzy you see, first she's a baby, ah, then a schoolgirl, ahm, then a teenager, then ah, she gets married.' This went on until poor old Suzy gave up the ghost, died, went to heaven and goodness knows what else.

'But how do you actually play it?' I insisted.

'Well', she rolled her eyes again. 'We *actually* play it when we stand and hold hands – then we all sing:

> 'When Suzy was a baby,
> A baby Suzy was,
> She went Umh Umh, Umh Umh Umh.'

The first two lines were accompanied by a kind of communal hand-clapping, while the final Umh's were executed with the thumb being sucked, signifying the baby. She took a break here and had another mouthful.

'And then?' I urged.

'You'll give her indigestion,' Lynn said – Mums always say that!

'And then?' I repeated.

She went into the second verse.

> 'When Suzy was a schoolgirl,
> A schoolgirl Suzy was,
> She went, "Hey Miss, I can't do this."'

This time, the final line suggested Suzy's trying to attract the teacher's attention by raising her hand aloft. She picked up her spoon, at the same time smiling at me, knowing what was coming.

'And then?' I shouted, this time.

She laughed and gave the eyes another roll.

> 'When Suzy was a teenager,
> A teenager Suzy was,
> She said, "Ooh aah, I lost my bra,
> I left my knickers in my boyfriend's car."'

There was a sort of temporary paralysis for a few seconds, except for Fiona, who got back to the cornflakes.

'She said what?' Lynn asked, her eyebrows raised an extra inch or so.

Without even batting an eyelid, Fiona gave a repeat performance:

> 'She said, "Ooh aah, I lost my bra,
> I left my knickers in my boyfriend's car."'

'Are those the proper words?' Lynn's voice had also gone up a bit by now.

'Oh yes, that's what we sing,' said the young innocent.

'And do the sisters hear you sing that?' I joined in.

'Oh yes, Daddy, the sisters all know it!'

I looked at Lynn and trying not to laugh, was unable to resist the temptation. I said, 'Those are funny words, I think . . . "Ooh aah, I lost my bra, I left my knickers in my boyfriend's car". I don't understand them – I mean – what would Suzy be doing, taking off her knickers in her boyfriend's car?'

The eyes gave a few extra rolls this time – she'd obviously given no thought whatever to the lyric before. Then, slowly and thoughtfully, she said, 'Ahm, I don't know what she was doing really – perhaps she was changing for ballet.'

One of the unique things about these little 'out of the mouths of babes' stories, is that somehow, they can't be written by scriptwriters. They must simply happen. Here's another:

One lovely summer morning, while on a visit to my home town of Waterford in Ireland, I stood with my sister in the kitchen of her home, having a chat and sipping a cup of tea. The window to the tiny garden was open, and we could hear clearly the conversation of the children outside. We became aware that they were re-enacting some TV movies. As you would expect on these occasions, one of them had taken it upon himself to undertake the role of producer/director. We moved a bit nearer to the window. There stood the young Cecil B. De Mille, calmly instructing his cast as to their contribution. This was done, I might add, with great authority and with an Irish accent. The setting, as so often happens with young lads especially, was a western town.

'Tell you what,' he announced, turning to his brother. 'You be the sheriff, OK? You come galloping into town from up there – get off your horse and tie

Ronnie Corbett and Fatbelly Doonican on Ronnie's show, early 70s

Spot the ball?

Golfing with Mr Crosby, 1975

Dressed up for a garden party, Torquay, 1975

Two wandering minstrels – Cribbins and Doonican

A cosmopolitan folk song with Nana Mouskouri (representing Greece), myself (Ireland), Rolf Harris (Australia) and Roger Whittaker (Kenya) ·

All dressed up for Christmas with Twiggy and Roy Castle, late 70s

Wing Commander Wallis and I ready for take off

Lynn and I relaxing during a filming trip in Ireland

Yvonne Littlewood and myself with Perry Como, Christmas 1984

With choral director Ray Charles, 1983

Doonican and Denver

Playing *Last of the Summer Wine* with Ruth Madoc

Me and the Prime Mimicker, Janet Brown, Christmas 1985

Pat Boone and I being serenaded by James Galway, Christmas 1985

Fiona assisting Paul Daniels at
rehearsals for my show, 1985

Lynn and I at home

The Doonicans now!

him up by the shed . . . then you push open the doors of the saloon.' The sheriff nodded acceptance and adjusted his gun belt a bit. The director went on, this time pointing at the little lad from next door, ''Im and me will be playing cards and you pull your gun on us,' and so it went on. Eventually, they were about ready to 'do a take', as we say, when the lad from next door thought he should get something straight.

'Who are you and me supposed to be?' he asked. The lad in authority thought for a second or two and then announced:

'Tell you what, you can be Alias and I'll be Smithn Jones.'

More recently, my sister told me a delightful remark made by one of her neighbour's children. Mother busied herself about the house while the little lad, kneeling on one of the dining chairs, watched what was happening outside. Suddenly he shouted from his look-out position.

'Hey, Mammy, quick, have a look – there's a dog out here with high heels on.'

Mom walked to the window, and there, nibbling the grass across the road, was a goat. That's one of my favourite stories right now. Only a little lad could think of such an apt description of something he'd never really seen before. They manage to bring things down to basics in a way that's peculiar to them.

Some years back, I was involved in the making of a special album, the proceeds of which were to be given to the charitable organisation UNICEF. As part of the promotion, it was arranged that the first copy was to be purchased by, and presented to, the Prime Minister. Mr Edward Heath held that office at the time, and a visit to No. 10 Downing Street was organised, complete with the usual batch of press photographers. We were asked to go as a family, so naturally the girls were dressed up for the occasion. On arrival we were ushered into one of the large reception rooms used for those functions. It was beautifully furnished, and the floor was covered in a magnificent Persian-style carpet. The two girls, who were aged about five and six at the time, had strict instructions not to touch anything, so while waiting for the arrival of our very special contributor, they began to play a kind of 'hopscotch' game with the designs on the carpet. When Mr Heath eventually came in, he greeted everybody very courteously, giving extra attention to his young guests.

'Do you like our nice house?' he said to them. Once again everything was brought back to the basics, they smiled their approval and then Sarah issued a challenge to the Prime Minister.

'I'll bet,' she said, pointing to the carpet, 'that you can't get from here to there without treading on the blue bits.'

Needless to say, he didn't try it at that moment. In fact, he was preparing to meet a deputation from the Miners' Union immediately after our visit, so a much more complex game of hopscotch was on the horizon.

Wild cactus – this one was fifteen feet high

—— Chapter Five ——

In 1970, I had the pleasure of being one of the chosen subjects for TV's *This Is Your Life*. I can honestly say that I didn't have a clue until that fateful moment when the little book was pushed in front of me, and those now famous words were addressed to me: 'Val Doonican, tonight, this is your life.' Unbeknown to me, the planning stages of the whole thing had been going on for ages beforehand. I truly suspected nothing, although after the deed had been perpetrated, I found myself putting all kinds of two and two's together.

The first question the organisers put to Lynn was, 'How can we be sure to catch him?'

'On the golf course,' she assured them. 'Organise an attractive game of golf with people he likes to play with, and come hail, rain or snow, he'll be there.'

That year, in fact, was a very special year for me professionally. I was now booked in my own show for a period of six months at the famous London Palladium. All kinds of plans were in the melting pot.

The family and I had just got back from holiday in Barbados, when I received a call from my agent. It appeared that Leslie Grade's office, who were responsible for staging the Palladium show, wished to talk to me about organising a special photographic session. The resulting photos were intended for the theatre souvenir brochure. I rang Leslie Grade (father of Michael Grade, now with BBC Television) who suggested I might like a round of golf with the famous Ryder Cup captain Dai Rees. A photographer, of course, would be in attendance to take some suitable shots. This all sounded very plausible to me, since my golfing routine with Norman Vaughan was well known.

The golf match was planned for a few weeks hence, and naturally I looked forward to it very much. I still had no inkling that this was part of a set-up. Now, believe it or not, only days before my golfing appointment, I had a phone call at about dinner time (Lynn was sitting, looking at a magazine, waiting for the food to be ready). The voice on the other end sounded very Irish. Frankly, I thought it was somebody trying to be funny. Mr Jimmy Tarbuck had done something similar on previous occasions. The conversation went something like this:

ME: 'Hello.'

VOICE: 'Can I speak to Val Doonican.'

ME: 'Speaking, who is this?'

VOICE: (a very Irish name).

ME: 'Sorry, how did you get this number [which is ex-directory]?'

VOICE: 'Oh, I'm with the *Irish Times* – we had it here in the office.'

ME: 'Is that you, Tarbuck?'

VOICE: 'Mr Doonican, could you tell me what you're doing next Wednesday?'

ME: 'Next Wednesday? Why do you ask that? I'm playing golf actually.'

VOICE: 'With Dai Rees.'

ME: 'Yes. How did you know that?'

VOICE: 'Actually, somebody tipped us off that it was Dai Rees' *This Is Your Life*. He's being set up!'

ME: 'Well, if he is, nobody's told me.'

VOICE: 'I see, well, thank you very much.'

I put the phone down, still wondering what the whole thing was about, and not suspecting a thing. Lynn looked up from her book. 'Who was that?'

I shook my head. 'No idea, says he's from some paper, asked me if next Wednesday is Dai Rees' *This Is Your Life.*'

Lynn put down her magazine. 'Potatoes are ready,' she said, disappearing into the kitchen. The whole thing disappeared from my mind. My friend Mickey rang me the next day, offering to take me to South Herts Golf Course on the Wednesday. I wondered why he'd want to come along, and consequently asked him.

'I'd love to meet Dai Rees,' he said convincingly, 'maybe get a picture of him.'

He picked me up on the Wednesday, with lots of time in hand. 'I thought we'd leave early,' he said, 'the traffic is pretty awful today.' In fact, we were just approaching the golf club, with about half an hour to spare, when Mickey suddenly said, 'I'll take you down this way, there are some fantastic houses in this road. We've plenty of time anyway.'

I said that I wouldn't mind being early. 'Give me a chance to hit a few shots and loosen up.'

Undaunted, Mickey showed me all the houses as if he had just become an estate agent. He'd obviously been told to get me there at a certain time, in order to avoid my seeing any scanner vans from Thames TV which were secreting themselves in the vicinity of the clubhouse.

Dai was his charming self, the photographer was eager and ready, so things began to happen. We made our way to the teeing ground and our round began.

Once again, it was easy to deduce, in retrospect, that Dai had been asked to have me on the eighteenth green at a certain time. At the time, however, I was covered in confusion. We'd played some nine or ten holes when he casually suggested that we cut across the adjacent tee and play back towards the clubhouse. 'Looks as if it's going to pour down,' he said, looking up into a pretty rainless sky. Anyway, we'd had quite a few pictures and I thought maybe the great man had better things to do and had given quite enough of his valuable time.

Soon we were playing our approach shots on to the eighteenth green. In fact, I played quite a good one, which was followed by Dai's shot, on this occasion not quite as close to the flag as mine. (I'll elaborate on this in a moment.)

The eighteenth green is quite elevated at South Herts, and as we popped our heads above the hill approaching it, I noticed a man standing by the flag, wearing a golf hat. 'What's he doing there?' I thought as I approached my ball, then like a bolt from the blue, I recognised Eamonn Andrews. 'Eamonn!' I exclaimed, 'What the hell are you doing here?' Then as if struck by a thunderbolt, I thought, 'My God, it *is* Dai's *This Is Your Life*.' Dai, Mickey and myself gathered round Eamonn, and I waited in anticipation for Dai's shattering surprise. Then it came:

'Val Doonican, tonight, this is your life.'

It really was a wonderful night. The only occasion in about thirty-five years when the entire Doonican family (with the exception of my father) were gathered together in one room. Some of my dearest friends came from far and wide, together with some special people from show business, in particular the late Dickie Henderson, and Moira Anderson, who was appearing in the Palladium show.

One lovely surprise brought very special memories of my boyhood back in Ireland. When I was very young, in common with most other boys, I longed for the weekly treat of Saturday at the pictures. I just loved cowboys – one of my favourites being Gene Autry. Lynn knew that I had written to him when I was about six years of age, asking for his autograph. Sadly, I never had a reply. Well, half-way through my evening of surprises, there on film, direct from his home in America, was the legendary Mr Autry himself.

'Howdy there, Val,' he greeted me, while leaning on a corral gate. 'Gee, I'm sure glad to have this opportunity of sending my greetings to you, and to apologise most sincerely for not answering your letter.'

That was followed by a short extract from one of his movies. 'And that,' said Eamonn, 'was what you and Mickey paid your precious fourpence to see way back in those early days.'

'Jesus,' said Mickey, 'we were robbed.'

Well, as I've said, it's easy to be wise after the event, and think 'I should have twigged that something was going on'. For example, during our West Indies holiday, Lynn had about four long-distance calls from London, making up all kinds of stories as to who they were from; there had been that strange phone call from the phantom Irish man, Mickey's sightseeing trip around South Herts, and Dai's ending the round of golf so quickly.

Two memorable remarks were made at the party afterwards. I told Eamonn that I took great exception to his opening comments on film, spoken, incidentally, over the arrival of our two balls on to the eighteenth. Since we were not in view, you simply saw an empty green, then a ball pitching on. As I've said earlier, my ball arrived first, quite close to the flag. 'Oh, that'll be Dai,' says Eamonn's voice, then Dai's ball appeared, not quite so close. 'Yes, that'll be Val.' The cheek of the man.

The second story came from an ex-member of the Four Ramblers. I hadn't seen Tommy Burns for about fifteen years, but he'd been flown across from Dublin. It so happens that my family were on the same plane. My mother, however, was travelling incognito, using the name Mrs O'Reilly (this was just a precaution in case anybody noticed that there was a Mrs Doonican on the plane, and mentioned it to me). My old partner Tommy, however, had known my mother for many years and recognised her, but wasn't sure if she'd remember him – after all, she was then 82. As they disembarked in London, some representatives from Thames TV greeted them. As they were all going to spend some time together as a party, introductions were considered advisable. Tommy was just about to say hello to my mother when somebody said to him, 'Oh Mr Burns, have you met Mrs O'Reilly?' He was a bit lost for words, and remarked to me later:

'I had no idea your mother had married again.'

One of the most common questions asked by young journalists who interview you about your career is, 'What was your most embarrassing moment?' Now, strange to say, I find it difficult to give any kind of memorable examples. Considering the amount of live TV I've done in my career, it amazes me how few things have, in fact, gone disastrously wrong.

Back in the sixties I remember one evening having among my guests that brilliantly talented ventriloquist Ray Alan, with his notorious partner, Lord Charles. Well, the show went just fine as far as I recall, until I made my closing announcement. I thanked all my guests, ending with, 'My thanks also to Mr Ray Alan and his friend *Ray* Charles.' Now, simply saying Ray Charles instead of Lord Charles would not have been too much of a disaster had there not been a world famous entertainer of that name. All through the following week I was constantly reminded of what I had said, so in an effort to end the whole thing, I decided to apologise on the following Saturday. Having gone through the closing speech I added, 'Oh, by the way, may I just acknowledge the goof I made last Saturday at the end of the show. I referred to Lord Charles as Ray Charles. So, my apologies to Lord Charles, and although I'm pretty sure that Ray Charles wasn't watching, I apologise for taking his name in vain.'

I smiled and said goodnight as we went off the air. As is customary, I then returned to the studio floor just to thank the audience for coming along. Everybody was laughing. The floor manager came out to see me. 'That's what I call out of the frying pan and into the fire,' he said. Only then did it dawn on me what I had said in that closing announcement: 'I'm pretty sure Ray Charles wasn't watching.' 'God,' I thought, 'Ray Charles is blind!' I decided to leave well enough alone after that, but was truly astonished at the number of viewers who thought I actually meant it as some kind of sick joke.

Having known many blind people over the years, I

feel quite sure that Ray Charles would have been the last person to take offence at the remark. Blind people who come to my concerts think nothing of saying, 'It's the first time I've seen you live,' or 'We watch you every Saturday night.'

Back in the fifties, while I was working with the Ramblers, we appeared one night on a Saturday variety show at the Winter Gardens in Margate. Topping the bill were Terry Scott and Hugh Lloyd working as a double act. Also appearing were those veterans of the Music Hall, usually identified by the phrase 'Play the game, cads, play the game' – the Western Brothers. On this particular occasion there was no compère to introduce the entire show. The manager came backstage carrying a copy of the show's running order, and asked each act in order of appearance if, at the conclusion of their spot, they would kindly introduce the following turn. Since we were a quartet, one of us had to take on this little chore. I drew the short straw and at the end of our act, returned to the microphone. My partners stood watching from the wings, as I nervously prepared my speech.

'And now, ladies and gentlemen, it is my pleasure to introduce two men who have been household names for many years. If I simply say "Play the game you cads", you will of course know that I can only say – Please welcome' – and horror of horrors my mind went blank. After what seemed an interminable gap, I blurted out 'Bob and Alf Pearson'. The last thing I heard through the rather hesitant applause that followed was the furious voice of one of the Western Brothers coming from behind the curtains, shouting:

'What did that bloody young fool say?'

The Four Ramblers must have broken all records that night for packing up and vacating the theatre.

There was no way I could have come face to face with these two gentlemen after such an unforgivable blunder.

In 1972 I signed a new record contract, this time with the Phonogram Company, better known to you, the record-buying public, as Philips. I'd previously been with the Pye label, and before that, under contract to Decca. Since, as I've told you, all my previous recordings remained the joint property of Eve and myself, we were now able to pass them on to Phonogram for the duration of our contract, to do with as they wished. They immediately set about releasing several compilations of previously released tracks, including a six-box set marketed by the Readers' Digest Company.

Having spent the summer of 1971 working on the American TV shows, it was back to summer season again in 1972, the venue on this occasion being the Winter Gardens in Bournemouth.

I joined Parkstone Golf Club for the season, and enjoyed my free time with friends and members at this very hospitable club. My own golf reached its peak around that time, I think: I began to achieve very consistent low scores, and was quite proud of myself for acquiring a handicap of four. I know that this kind of information means nothing to the non-golfer, but for me and my hobby at the time, it was everything.

Speaking of non-golfers, I came home from Parkstone Golf Club one day, having played in a match and returned a score of level par. I was absolutely elated as I walked through the kitchen door.

'Hi love,' I shouted.

'Hello,' Lynn answered from the lounge, 'have a good morning?'

'Good morning?' I asked mockingly. 'A good morning? Do you know that I played in a match this morning and I *had a par round*?'

She went on with whatever she was doing. 'Bully for you then,' she said, 'is that good?'

'It only means that I didn't drop a single shot.' I thought that was bound to get some kind of recognition. I waited.

Finally she spoke. 'Oh, by the way love, the office rang. Will you give them a buzz before five?' and that was that. If our marriage could survive that, believe me it could survive anything!

Later that year I did my first home-grown series of shows, as well as a Christmas special, for ATV, and enjoyed myself much more. Looking through my diary for the year that followed makes me realise what energy and enthusiasm I had in those days. The sheer weight of my commitments had little or no effect on me at the time as far as I recall, which confirms the old saying 'amazing how time slips by when you're enjoying yourself'. The year began with a trip to Holland, followed by a season at the then famous Coventry Theatre in preparation for a long summer show at the ABC Theatre in Great Yarmouth. This was to be followed by a further eight weeks at the Prince of Wales Theatre in London, which, in turn, was followed by another television series. Many, many further entries clutter up my date book, all contributing to what surely must have been one of my busiest years.

As in the previous year, my golfing activities occupied every available moment away from the grindstone. My home club was Sandy Lodge in Middlesex, and I was very much part of its landscape week in, week out, whether playing friendly games, brushing up on my technique in the practice area or trying my skill in the many competitions. It was in one such competition that I acquired one of my most treasured possessions, now taking pride of place in my den at home: a large gold piece about the size of a sovereign, presented once a year to the winner of the club championship. It's called the scratch gold medal. I will not bore all of you non-golfers by describing what all that means, but I can truthfully say that it's the prize most keen golfers would love to achieve during their playing years at club level. I've got to admit that my score wasn't all that impressive, but nobody can take away the fact that it was the best score returned over two rounds on that particular course, with all the best players taking part. Seeing my name entered in gold on the club champions' board inside the lounge made all my hard work and determination worthwhile. I had for some time been part of the club's first team, representing Sandy Lodge in matches against such visiting groups as Oxford, Cambridge and London Universities, and managed to put up a reasonable show on these occasions in spite of being much older than most of my opponents. In fact, those young lads weren't even born when I began playing back in the early fifties, and I was then in my twenties.

I knew that my television shows were being sold to various English-speaking countries around the world. Like many British-based artists, I was attracting interest from a lot of them, in particular, Australia and New Zealand. The extent of the shows' popularity, however, was a bit uncertain. I just knew that people were seeing them, and for this I was grateful. It was also helping record sales abroad.

Enquiries began to come in as to the possibility of a tour 'down under', but while my success at home was still relatively untapped, Eve kept putting it off. I simply didn't have the time to take on any more engagements. By the beginning of the seventies, the time appeared to be right, so a tour was arranged, beginning with some twenty or so appearances in

New Zealand, followed by five or six weeks in Australia.

The summer prior to the tour saw me in summer season down in Bournemouth. One of my golfing partners during the engagement was Max Bygraves, who was also working there for that particular season, and lived there on a permanent basis. Max, one of the most experienced of all our top entertainers, had by that time undertaken several tours of the Antipodes, so I asked him what he thought my prospects might be.

'Oh, you'll love it mate, and you'll do fine,' Max assured me. 'They're a smashing audience. You might get the odd heckler when you work the clubs. They can quite enjoy having a go at the Poms, but don't let it worry you, each time you go over there you'll find it gets better and better.'

How right he was. I've been some eight times now over the years, and it's gradually become like a second home to me. The larger clubs over there, by the way, are mainly in the state of New South Wales, the only state where poker machines are legal. You'll find thousands of them throughout the clubs, their income being the main source of subsidy for the more expensive cabaret acts. The management of the more successful establishments come in three categories:

Leagues Clubs, run by the big Rugby League teams.

RSL Clubs, meaning Returned Servicemen's Leagues, and

The Workers' Clubs.

They can be quite huge concerns with thousands of members, their facilities appearing to know no bounds – two or three restaurants, catering for different tastes, indoor bowling greens, swimming pools, squash and tennis courts, discos for the young set, several bars, snooker rooms and, of course, a large cabaret room/concert hall, seating up to seventeen hundred people.

Engagements in the other states – Queensland, South Australia, Victoria, Western Australia, Northern Territories and Tasmania – are mainly confined to straightforward concerts. Personally speaking, my heart has always remained firmly devoted to the concert stage. So, through the years, my promoters have tended to book me more and more in that direction.

Well, with this exciting prospect on the horizon, my musicians, singers and I boarded a Qantas 747 at Heathrow, and embarked on our twelve thousand mile journey. The flight took us through the Middle East, then Hong Kong, and finally the last leg of the trip towards Australia.

Very weary and cramped, we made a brief pause in Melbourne, in the state of Victoria, and were escorted into the VIP lounge for refreshments. My travelling manager, Mickey, and I sat sipping a coffee, when a man sitting in a nearby chair caught my eye.

'G'day,' he said, winking. 'I think maybe I know your face.'

'You could be right,' I said, hoping he was not mistaking me for somebody else.

'Aren't you that "Val Something" fella who sings on the television?' he asked.

'That's right,' I told him.

'My wife watches you a bit,' he said, rather grudgingly. 'Are you over here for a holiday?'

Hell of a way for a holiday, I thought to myself. 'I'm on my way to New Zealand,' I explained, 'to do some shows.' He looked at me a bit taken aback.

'You're not thinking of working here in Oz, are you?' he said, almost threateningly.

I was tempted to say no, and end the conversation. I didn't like the sound of it, but I told the truth.

'As a matter of fact, yes, I am, in a couple of weeks or so.' I waited.

'Well you're a brave man I would have thought,' he said. 'I can't imagine you being popular enough for that.'

Well, there's nothing like a bit of encouragement at the start of a new venture.

My eventual arrival in Auckland, New Zealand, turned out to be a memorable occasion. In spite of my physical exhaustion, and longing for a comfortable bed, great celebrations seemed to be in progress as we disembarked near the arrival terminal. Huge crowds of people were gathered, waving and cheering, and a group of young people in some kind of traditional costume sang and danced on the tarmac surface adjoining the airport building. All my company and I wondered what the occasion could be, and looked around for a clue, never thinking for one moment that the centre of attraction was, in fact, myself. As we walked from the aircraft, the crowd's enthusiasm became even more pronounced, while on closer investigation the traditional costumes worn by the young dancers turned out to be Irish.

This, of course, was a totally new experience for me, my career up to that time, and indeed since, having gone along at a steady, but low-key pace.

Inside the terminal block, hordes of waiting people greeted me with warm words of welcome, before I was whisked away to my hotel for a press conference. All my tiredness and jet-lag seemed to fade with the sincerity of the hospitality extended to me over the next couple of hours. When at last I retired to my hotel suite, I slept for goodness knows how long.

The tour was to be a remarkable one in my experience. Each evening, the packed houses, the crowds awaiting my arrival at the concert halls, not to mention those waiting to see me afterwards, continued to amaze me. I simply had no idea of the extent of my popularity in this little country some twelve thousand miles from the BBC Television Studios in London.

I recall a visit to a local radio station where I was to do an interview. I discovered that only with a police escort could our car get into the street where the station was situated. Until that time, I'd associated such public reaction with young pop idols such as Cliff Richard or David Cassidy, or the Beatles, but never with a middle-aged family entertainer such as myself.

Well, the tour lived up to all expectations, with not a single seat available at any one of the twenty or so performances.

This happened, by the way, during a period when my working attire was mainly confined to what Lynn liked to describe as elegant casuals. The habit of my being dressed in a well-chosen wardrobe of knitwear was something, which, like the rocking-chair, had crept up on me, so to speak, eventually becoming an integral part of my television personality.

Since the climate in Australia was not the ideal one for such stagewear, it was decided that we'd have some custom-built lightweight casuals made by a well known London men's store. (I might add that I never intended, at any time, to wear casual clothes on stage. They were strictly a TV idea, originally chosen for their design rather than colour, since the first four or five series I did were in black and white. However, the popularity of the idea was such that had I not made some effort at following it through on stage, the audience, somehow, would have felt a bit cheated.) It was recommended by the makers of these specially designed pieces, that they should be very carefully hand-washed, something which became quite an issue during a hectic tour of one night stands. There was a memorable occasion when we played a concert at one of the large venues, which was followed by a well-earned day off. The only problem facing me was that my stagewear needed to be washed and cleaned, but our day off happened to be a Sunday.

Our audience for the Saturday concert included a party of sisters from a local convent. My manager, Mickey, on having a word with them, discovered that several of them originated from the vicinity of our home town in Ireland. After the show, we invited them backstage for a chat. An unusual occurrence for them, I feel sure. They admired my stage sweaters, which prompted Mickey to mention our cleaning problem. Without the slightest hesitation, they enthusiastically offered their assistance, suggesting that they should take the sweaters away, promising to have them all clean and ready by the following afternoon. The only condition facing me was that I had to agree to go to the convent the next afternoon for tea, whilst at the same time collecting my laundry.

Well, they gave us a wonderful welcome the next day, and a sumptuous tea was laid before myself and my associates. As so often happens on these kind of visits, a guitar eventually appeared from behind a sofa, and was discreetly moved in my direction. An hour long sing-song with a strong Irish bias was to follow.

The sisters, armed with their personal cameras, took endless souvenir photographs of our enjoyable visit, copies of which, I feel sure, were to make their way across the Irish Sea during the following weeks.

My stagewear never had such devoted care and attention, or smelled as clean and wholesome as after it had been looked after by the kindly laundresses. A delightful footnote to the occasion was later passed on to me by one of the girls in our group. It appears the sisters had some second thoughts about their generous offer while returning home after the show.

'Suppose they were stolen from the clothes line behind the convent,' one of them said, 'what on earth would we do? They couldn't possibly be replaced.' They obviously viewed the possibility quite seriously, too, as the upshot of their concern was a decision to take turns at a kind of sentry duty. Their vigil went on until the clothes were dry. For the remainder of the tour, my stage attire became affectionately known among our group as 'Doonican's Habits'.

So, I was sad indeed to say goodbye to the people of New Zealand. We boarded the plane and waved our farewells, hoping deep down that Australia would not turn out to be something of an anti-climax.

We stopped off at Sydney, en route to Melbourne, where our first Australian concert was to take place. We then planned to return to Sydney, where I was to appear at one of the top clubs for a month's engagement. The entertainment manager of the club in question kindly met us in Sydney, simply to say how much he was looking forward to our visit and happily to inform us that the entire month's engagement was sold out.

The Australian section of the tour was just as exciting an experience for the company, and we all looked forward to the prospect of being invited to repeat the trip. (In fact, I can honestly say that I enjoy it more and more as the years go by.)

In common with so many of my fellow 'workaholics', I've never been all that enamoured by the prospect of going away on holiday. I've loved it from the family's point of view, of course, and look back on our many trips, when the children were younger, with great affection. Now, as I get a little older and the pressure of work has greatly decreased, I find that my attitude towards going away for a break is fast approaching what it should have been all along. Up to the time when Lynn and I got married, in fact, I'd never really bothered to go on holiday at all. I suppose I thought my work was like a never-ending vacation.

It has been suggested to me on occasions, that perhaps I never found the right kind of holiday for me personally. Who knows, maybe my 'ideal' is waiting somewhere out there and we simply haven't got together. I should clarify the situation by saying that I love just staying at home, using the time to catch up on my hobbies. In recent times we've acquired a little holiday home abroad, and I intend using its peace and quiet to make up for my lost time. I want to read all those good books that I never got round to because of my busy life.

My initiation into the more exotic kind of holidays came about in the mid-sixties through some friends of ours. The husband had achieved quite exceptional success with the company for which he worked, and was invited by them to spend some time in the West Indies as their manager there. Before leaving, the family kindly invited Lynn and me to come out and spend a holiday there as their guests, whenever we felt like it. Since we were busy settling into our new home at the time, we felt the idea to be a bit out of reach financially. Fortunately my career was coming along in leaps and bounds, and pretty soon we began viewing the idea as a real possibility.

The following winter found us both enjoying the warm sunshine of Jamaica, not to mention the warmth of hospitality extended to us by Terry and his wife Bobbie, and their young family. After that initial introduction we made regular visits with our girls to both Jamaica and Barbados, sharing the joys of the Caribbean with fellow members of the entertainment world, like Harry and Myra Secombe, David and Barbara Coleman and their respective families.

One sunny morning Harry, David and I went on a

Rubber tree

deep sea fishing trip. An elegant cabin cruiser with a crew consisting of two young lads came and picked us up from the beach adjoining our hotel.

'Well, Val, old son,' I thought climbing over the side, 'this is a hell of a long way from the piece of string, bent pin, and tin of worms. This is the real stuff.'

The young skipper, inviting us to make ourselves comfortable, began pouring three very generous beakers of rum punch. Dressed in floppy sun hats, swimming shorts and little else, we settled down, sipping our local brew and wishing the folks at home could see us. Meanwhile our three fishing lines, baited and cast over the stern, were being made secure in the special housings which allowed them simply to get on with our job, as we headed seaward.

Each line has a little of its slack taken up before cast off. This is held securely by a kind of clothes peg device. At the first signs of tension on the line the slack is suddenly released, accompanied by a warning 'crack' as the peg snaps shut, signifying 'a bite'. That's usually the signal for novices such as myself to leap out of their seats, running madly about the place wondering what to do next. Then follows a most fascinating piece of theatre in my opinion. The young expert, with great enthusiasm, grabs the line and having invited you to jump into the work-seat to which your personal rod is attached he slowly and skilfully brings your fish home. All the time you're acting as a kind of willing helper, and sharing in the excitement. The job completed he pats you on the back and shouts, 'Well done, sah, you got 'im and he's a beauty, too.'

It's a wonderful morale booster, especially later as you stroll up the beach, a large kingfish slung over your shoulder.

I knew that Harry had done it all many times

before, so deep down I said a little prayer that the fish would pick him first, then I could sit and watch.

Goodness knows how many rum punches later Harry held the floor, or the deck, with endless stories of his days in the forces and his years with the Goons. Suddenly, we heard the warning click and one of the lines took up its slack. It was Harry's. He leaped into action, assisted by one of our young experts.

'Take it easy now, sah,' he said in his lovely West Indian accent. 'Don't rush him, sah.'

A huge kingfish leaped from the water, some distance from the boat, only to disappear again into the depths, while David and I watched, and shouted our encouragement. Well, whether it was a case of Harry doing all the right things, or the fish's being a bit of an amateur, I don't know, but in no time, we were pulling the gleaming catch on board. He was a beauty indeed, and I must say I felt a bit sorry for him as he thrashed about there on the floor in the stern of the boat.

Harry must have felt that sense of guilt also, 'cause no sooner had the kingfish shown signs of ending his struggle, then Harry took him by the fin and started apologising profusely.

'I'm sorry, my old lad,' he told him, 'it could have been any of them out there, you were just passing at the time. Nothing personal, you understand.'

The fish showed no sign whatever of accepting any excuses, but just lay there motionless. Then came Harry's final tribute to his victim. Holding the blue coloured tail between his palms and gazing out to sea, he burst into song in that rich tenor voice:

'Your tiny hand is frozen, let me warm it into life.'

His familiar tones echoed across the beautiful blue carpet of water with just the odd fish popping its head up to see what the hell was going on. David and I were busy laughing with Harry, never thinking for a moment that this was anything unusual for Mr Seagoon. Our laughter turned to hysterics, however, as we turned around and caught sight of our young 'captain and mate', and the look of total bewilderment on their faces. You can well imagine, two youngsters who didn't know Harry from Adam, standing there thinking he must have lost his mind.

'Who is that maan?' one of them asked, smiling. We smiled back, reassuring them that he was quite sane and did this sort of thing for a living. One of them turned to Harry and said, 'What's your name, sah?'

'Secombe,' shouted Harry.

'Where you come from, sah?' the lad asked. I knew what was coming next and couldn't wait to see the lad's face.

'I come from Wales,' Harry told him.

'Where, sah?' the boy said, looking puzzled: he'd obviously never heard of Wales.

'Wales,' Harry repeated, 'Wales, boy.' Then slapping his huge torso with the palms of his hands he said, 'With a figure like mine, I couldn't very well have come from Sardines, could I?' This was followed by the typical Secombe laugh and a raspberry. The young boy looked at all of us with a blank expression. They couldn't be expected to see the joke really. They'd probably never heard of a place called Sardines, either.

It's a very interesting study, actually trying to analyse how well certain types of humour will travel. Like wines, some will be acceptable on arrival, while others will just die in transit. Being Irish, and having been weaned on my own native humour, I've lived through countless examples of 'One man's humour being another man's blank look'. Phrases or sayings which were so much part of my early life, can, when casually introduced into a conversation, bring a snigger of approval from some, or nothing more than a puzzled look from others.

I appeared on television some years ago with a very successful international star. Part of our preliminary conversation was to be on the subject of poetry, and the art of writing lyrics for popular songs. I had mentioned, during a script meeting, that when I was a young lad, our prize chestnut was as follows:

> There was a young man from Tralee,
> Who was stung on the neck by a wasp.
> When asked if it hurt,
> He said, 'Not at all,
> He can do it again if he likes.'

The Americans present had never heard it before, thought it funny, and suggested that I include it in the chat. At rehearsals that afternoon I recited it in passing. One or two of the floor crew laughed out loud, but the star of the show just looked at me amazed. 'You're not going to say that are you?' he asked, 'It doesn't make sense, I mean, it doesn't even rhyme!'

I met a young lady in the fifties, who informed me that 'she wasn't very good at seeing jokes'. We were touring as a company by coach at the time, journeys lightened by the usual plethora of funny stories, rude or otherwise. The girl in question seemed to join in the fun just like the rest of us, so I naturally doubted her admission regarding her sense of humour. One of the other members of the Ramblers had a delightfully droll kind of wit which he displayed on many occasions during our travels.

Our show concluded, we boarded the bus one warm sticky night, everybody looking a bit drained. The young lady was last to climb on. Flicking the pretty blonde hair from her eyes she gasped, 'Cor, isn't it close tonight?'

Quick as flash my Irish friend piped up, ''Tis love, especially when you're up near it.' As one, the company chuckled their appreciation.

'What's so funny?' asked the blonde, looking puzzled.

I decided to act as interpreter. 'Well, you said, it's close tonight, and he said, 'tis, especially when you're up near it. Get it? *Close, near?'*

'Oh yeah,' she said laughing, but we all knew damn well that she had no idea what I was talking about. She was to prove it in the most engaging way some days later. We sat around the supper table enjoying a pre-show meal, when the waitress, looking a bit hot and bothered, commented, 'Phew, isn't it hot this evening?'

Our blonde friend couldn't resist the opportunity to retaliate. 'Yes, it is, love,' she jumped in, 'especially when you're up close to it.' Everybody round the table positively exploded, while the waitress, a blank expression on her face, said, 'What did I say that was funny?' Our young lady probably came to the conclusion that the serving lady couldn't see jokes either.

I enjoy most kinds of humour myself, from Woody Allen to Billy Connolly, Alan King to Les Dawson, Laurel and Hardy to Bill Cosby. It's an enviable talent, making people laugh, night after night, year in year out.

My second tour of Australia and New Zealand in 1974 turned out to be just as successful and enjoyable as the first, although the final few days were marred by a persistent nagging pain in the pit of my stomach. When finally I sought some medical help, I was informed that the cause of my discomfort was a hernia. 'I'd have that seen to as soon as you get back to London,' the doctor advised, 'it looks pretty bad to me.' In typical fashion my promise to heed his words faded away once the pain eased and I got back into the swing of things at home.

Shortly afterwards Roger and I were scheduled to fly over to Holland for a four day recording session. Both Lynn and Roger's wife Maureen agreed to join us, hoping to turn the trip into a kind of holiday. The last day of our visit happened to coincide with the birthday of Queen Juliana of the Netherlands, with many of the popular eating places inviting their customers to partake of a celebratory dinner in the lady's honour. It was quite late in the evening when Roger and myself, feeling hungry, thirsty and exhausted, joined the girls at a very elegant restaurant in the city centre. Tragically for me, however, as the evening went by I began to feel those dreaded stomach pains again, only on this occasion they were to get more and more severe, till I thought it best to step outside for some fresh air.

By now the pain was such that I was feeling a bit unsteady and staggered slightly as I left the table. Before I could regain my balance, a powerfully strong hand gripped my arm, while the gentle voice of the head waiter whispered in my ear, 'I'm sorry sir, but I'm afraid I'll have to ask you to leave.' Then, looking around as if trying not to make a scene, he continued, 'You've obviously had far too much to drink . . .'

In spite of my discomfort I felt absolutely furious with the man, and pulling my arm free of his vice-like grip, said, 'What are you talking about . . . too much to drink?' But before I could say more I once again lost my balance, this time ending up on my knees.

The waiter, accompanied by an irate Mrs Doonican, then escorted me to the reception area outside where Lynn called for a taxi to take me back to our hotel. Funnily enough our waiter friend showed no further interest in the proceedings, disappearing through the doors to resume his duties in the dining-room.

Some thirty minutes or so later I lay on my bed, while a local medical man checked me over, only to repeat the familiar message, 'I should get home as quickly as you possibly can and have that attended to.' He then went on to inform me that I'd developed what's known as a strangulated hernia, which needed immediate attention.

Within a couple of days news of my emergency surgery made all the British newspapers. Roger popped in to see me at the nursing home . . . 'I hope that head waiter hears about this,' he joked. 'He'll be shocked to find what we do to drunks over here in London.'

It was a welcome surprise to discover that my return to the Opera House in Blackpool that summer was to coincide once again with the staging of the British Open Golf Championship at Royal Lytham Golf Club. To many of my golfing friends it began to look as though my bookings were far more influenced by the Royal and Ancient (the governing body of golf) than by my own professsional advisors.

The young Tony Jacklin, who had thrilled us with his sensational victory back in 1969, was by now quite the golfing superstar, having added the US Open Golf Championship to his list of victories. In fact, I was invited to appear in a television transmission from the golf course just before the British Open got under way. The BBC show *Nationwide* did a special edition of their programme, viewing the game of golf from many different angles.

Michael Barrett, Sue Lawley and Bob Wellings each covered one facet of the sport – Michael interviewing Gary Player on the question of technique, obtaining a short lesson in the process; Tony Jacklin speaking to Bob Wellings about the business side; and myself having the pleasure of chatting to Sue Lawley about the joys of golf as a pastime for us itinerant entertainers.

149

We were treated to another magnificent feast of golf that week, and as far as I recall Gary Player took the honours in a most exciting finish.

It's worth mentioning the fact that my season turned out to be yet another very successful one.

The summer of 1975 found us back in Torquay, and what a happy time that turned out to be. I was appearing at the Princess Theatre, while Ronnie Corbett starred at the Festival Theatre in Paignton, just down the road. Another friend, comedian Jerry Stevens, was staging his own show at one of the major hotels. Ronnie, Jerry, my friend Mickey and I made up one of the most enjoyable golfing partnerships I can remember. Just about every morning of the week we made our way to Newton Abbot Golf Club, known to most people as 'Stover', to enjoy a four-ball match followed by a snack lunch and a drink. The club made us very welcome, as indeed do most golf clubs around the country.

Ronnie's daughters Sophie and Emma were about the same age as Sarah and Fiona, which was fortunate. Lynn and Ronnie's wife Anne took them to the beach on many occasions while we were at the golf club, or having an afternoon nap prior to our two evening performances. A mutual friend of ours named Mervin Saunders had the use of a very nice boat, and frequently took us out as a family. Complete with picnic lunch we travelled along the coast enjoying the sunshine, at the same time getting a welcome respite from the bustle of the busy holiday town. One Sunday, the Corbetts and ourselves were returning from such a trip when the children's attention centred on a huge oil tanker, standing off the bay some distance out to sea. 'Could we go and have a look at it?' they asked. We tried to explain just how far away it was, but they persisted with their request.

Both the 'Dads' were quite adamant, however. It was our friend Mervin who finally brought the subject to a head.

'Oh come on,' he said, turning the wheel seaward, 'it's not all that far.' Well, it was 'all that far', in fact, but worth the trip. I'd never believe that a vessel could be so huge, and, never having experienced one so close to, I was very impressed. We did a couple of circuits of the ship and headed for home.

By strange coincidence, I attended a cocktail party the following week and was introduced to someone who was very much involved in the world of oil tankers. He was, however, much more fascinated by our world of summer entertainment.

'How many shows a week do you do?' he enquired.

'Twelve,' I told him. He looked surprised.

'Gosh, twelve shows a week, for how long?'

'About four months, I suppose,' I said.

'What?' he gasped. 'That's ... Let me see ... Crikey, almost two hundred shows. You must be positively knackered at the end of that lot.'

I tried to explain that it's just a job of work, and you get used to it.

'You must have one hell of a holiday when you've finished it,' he said, shaking his head.

'Just a couple of weeks, in fact,' I admitted, 'then I start work on a TV series.' The expression on his face was such that I began to feel ashamed.

'Two weeks is no damn good.' He was more or less telling me off now. 'You should have a month or two.'

I laughed out loud. 'I haven't had two months off for as long as I remember.'

'Well, you should have,' he said, beginning to sound like my family doctor. 'You can't possibly recharge your batteries in two weeks.' Then taking me by the arm, he guided me towards the window overlooking the bay. 'See that tanker out there,' he said, pointing towards the horizon. I nodded into my glass of wine. 'Well, you and I are no different from that monster. It takes ages really to get it moving, but it's even harder to bring it to a complete stop. You can switch off everything, but its own impetus will take it on for miles.'

'Miles?' I said, with an air of disbelief.

'Miles,' he repeated, 'and the first of those miles is about the same as your two weeks' holiday. You haven't even come to a halt when you're back to your TV series or whatever.'

I've thought quite a bit about that gentleman's words of wisdom. I think he's got something!

The daily rounds of golf were just what I needed that summer. Apart from the sheer joy that game brings anyway, I was both mentally and technically preparing myself for a very important game. I had been invited, some months previously, to take part in the very successful television series *Pro Celebrity Golf* at the beautiful Gleneagles Golf Club in Scotland. When the great day arrived I was picked up at all hours of the morning, from our temporary home on the outskirts of Torquay, and taken by road to Exeter airport. A small private aircraft was awaiting me there, and within ten minutes of my arrival, I was being whisked away in a northerly direction. Happily, the weather en route was glorious, so I just sat there enjoying the view and wondering what joys or disasters lay in store for me. The whole series of *Pro Celebrity Golf* is usually played over a couple of weeks, the promoters endeavouring to put two nine-hole matches 'in the can' per day. The pilot drew my attention to a tiny grass airstrip up ahead, or should I say down ahead, a long tidy row of similar aircraft to our own lining either side of it, rather like a guard of honour. Some black limousines stood by the modest reception buildings indicating, in fact, that I wasn't the only one arriving at that particular time. In fact, as I said hello to one of the representatives from BBC Television, standing by the cars, another plane lightly touched down. 'That'll be Mr Crosby now,' I heard somebody behind me say, causing my ears to prick up. One of my great personal ambitions had long been to meet the man I always considered to be the finest pop singer of all time. I felt sure the opportunity was at hand, knowing we were both heading for the same destination.

A minute or two later, I was ushered into one of the waiting cars, and just as I climbed aboard, a voice said, 'Oh Val, have you met Bing?' I turned, and there entering the car parked alongside was The Man Himself.

'Hi there Val, how'ya doin'?' he reached out of the car and took my hand. 'I believe we're playin' a bit of golf together today.' Till that moment, of course, I had no idea who my playing opponent was to be. Just as our respective cars were pulling away, he opened his window and called out. 'Let's have some lunch together before the game.' We did just that within the hour, and then made our way to the golf course. Bing, as most golfers will know, had been an extremely good amateur golfer, and even while in his early seventies he still played well. It was indeed a day I shall never forget, made even more memorable by the young Scottish lad I told you about earlier, who had no idea who the great Mr Crosby was when he asked for my autograph during the round.

I was to return to Gleneagles the following summer and have the pleasure of seeing Mr Crosby once again. It wasn't so long after when we heard the sad news of his sudden and fatal heart attack on a golf course in Spain. I know it's been said by many people, but it's so true nevertheless, that I doubt if he would have chosen any other place on earth to say farewell than on a golf course.

Recently, while signing an autograph book outside a concert hall in Melbourne, Australia, I caught sight of the greeting written on the adjoining page. 'To Liz, Best Wishes, Bing Crosby'.

'That's a nice one to have, Liz,' I said to the lady.

'Oh yes, I treasure it,' she answered, and popping her autograph book back into her handbag, remarked, 'I wonder if any of you well-known people have ever kept track of how many hundreds of thousands of autographs you must sign.' Well, I'm sure the figure would be quite staggering, at least for some.

I've always been puzzled by certain people in the public eye, who simply refuse to sign autographs. Some say that the practice of collecting signatures is quite nonsensical, while others, frankly, can't be bothered going to the trouble. I personally feel that if it gives people pleasure, then why not? It's never really that inconvenient.

Having said that I'm reminded of an incident back in the mid sixties. We'd just moved into our new home in Rickmansworth and were at the stage when we had to eat snack meals while seated around an upturned tea chest. Then, early on a Sunday morning, Lynn called up the stairs. 'Love, something's wrong with the plumbing, everything's bunged up.' I came downstairs, to discover that the problem was quite serious and needed immediate attention. Having phoned one or two plumbers and drawn a blank, I decided to tackle it myself. I lifted the large manhole in our front drive and discovered the cause of the trouble. It was not a pretty sight. After a laborious search through the garage and outhouses, I discovered a couple of rather ancient rods. Climbing down into the uninviting manhole, I began to use my very limited knowledge of the situation, at the same time getting myself in a rare old state. After what seemed like ages, I began to make some headway and things looked hopeful. I decided to give it everything I'd got, in a last frantic effort to clear the problem. Just at that moment, I heard a well-educated voice say:

'Excuse me, Mr Doonican.' Struggling to my feet, I looked up, and must have looked such a sight in an old overall and cap I'd found in the garden shed. Peering down at me was the most delightful young lady dressed in school uniform, complete with straw hat.

'Good morning,' I groaned. 'Can I help you, dear?' Bless her, it didn't take much intelligence for her to know that she'd caught me at a bad time.

'Sorry to bother you,' she said quietly, 'but would you kindly let me have your autograph?' Then, having second thoughts about the prospect of my having to climb out of the manhole, she went on. 'Or maybe I should come back later, I live close by.' I thought that was a great idea, and we arranged a time. I took extra care over my appearance later on when she returned. You can just imagine her first impressions, on seeing a real television personality up close.

It's nice to see the thrill that people get from meeting well-known personalities, and I do tend to become more aware of it when I see it through the eyes of my children. I've enjoyed meetings between my girls (and indeed my own family and friends) and stars who have appeared with me on television. This brief getting together can be very important to the persons concerned, and I think it should be encouraged. All the more reason for me to feel disappointed in colleagues who scorn the idea of signing autographs.

I was enjoying a Sunday lunch with some friends of mine, some years back. We were at a very popular hotel in Northern Ireland. My friends on this occasion consisted of a husband, wife and two young daughters who lived nearby. Midway through our meal, one of the daughters went quite wide-eyed and flustered, having spotted a very well known film actor at an adjoining table. Barely giving herself time to swallow her mouthful of food, she turned to her parents, and said excitedly, 'Mum, Dad, look who's over there. It's so-and-so.'

We all took a discreet look. 'You're right,' says Dad. 'It is him, but don't stare now, dear, just eat your lunch.' From that moment on, of course, neither of the girls could concentrate on their food, but continued to throw secretive glances in the direction of their film hero. Thinking me to be in the know about such situations, one of the girls asked:

'Do you think we could go and ask for his autograph, or would that be rude?'

'Well, I'm sure he wouldn't mind normally, but just the same, I would wait until he finishes his lunch.' I thought that this was the best I could do in the circumstances. They furtively watched while he finished his main course, then his dessert, and finally, ordered his coffee. As he sipped the latter, the girls thought it was time to give it another whirl.

'He might get up and leave when he finishes this, could we ask now?' The odd thing was, that when the time came to carry out their plan, both of them lost their nerve. 'You do it.' 'No, you ask him,' and so on, ending with 'Dad, will you ask him?'

I couldn't think of a more unlikely person to ask for an autograph from a film star than my friend, a very quiet, reserved kind of man. But he took the bull by the horns, picked up an old Sunday lunch menu from the table and left.

Excitedly, the girls watched his progress, while Mum and I looked on anxiously. Things couldn't have turned out worse. The star took exception to being approached and made his feelings quite clear. 'Damn it, man, can't you see I'm having lunch with friends? I wish people wouldn't be so rude as to come to my table', and so it went, until my friend, apologising and wishing the ground would open up and swallow him, returned to our table. Whatever the rights and wrongs of the situation may have been, I don't think it should have ended as it did. The ironic part was that as we left the restaurant, the gentleman in question recognised me and waved a very friendly greeting, while at the same time looking extremely sheepishly at my friend.

I've never appeared in pantomime as a solo artist. I specify 'solo artist', since I did appear many times while with the Ramblers, and found it great fun. Offers have come along, of course, but somehow, the idea of playing an Irish Robin Hood or Buttons just didn't appeal to me at all.

During my season at Torquay in 1975, I was invited to appear in a Christmas entertainment at the Opera House in Manchester. The show was never intended as any kind of pantomime, but simply a Festive Season Variety Show, scheduled to run for about eight weeks. In fact, the show was virtually the same as our Torquay bill, with the exception of one extra act, which had to be found.

My musical director, Roger, rang me one evening at home, saying he'd just been watching the show *Wheeltappers and Shunters*, and had seen an act on there which he felt would be ideal for our purposes, providing, of course, he was available and interested. During the following week, our show's producer, Maurice Fournier, put out some feelers and, in fact, managed to get a video of the act concerned. We all thought he was a great entertainer and ideal for our show. Fortunately, he was both available and interested, agreeing to join the show for rehearsals prior to our Manchester opening.

He was, as it turned out, a great asset to the show (his first ever theatre engagement, by the way), and was to appear with me for summer seasons over the two following years, in Scarborough in 1976 and Bournemouth in '77. The man I'm referring to is Paul Daniels, and from that first meeting in Manchester, somehow there was never any doubt he would achieve the success we've seen him enjoy since. Paul is a very inventive man with enormous drive and ambition. Then there's the talent and personality to make it all come together and work. I've really enjoyed watching his rise to the heights in recent years.

Having said all that, I must admit that the season at Manchester was not what I would call a hit. First and foremost, the audience didn't turn up in the kind of numbers I'd grown accustomed to seeing, and so again we get back to the argument as to why? The next season we did was everything I could ask for, so as I say, why? Maybe the show was not 'Christmassy' enough. Maybe the theatre was not the right venue for it. Maybe it was because Tommy Steele was having enormous success with his Hans Christian Andersen presentation just up the road at the Palace Theatre – or on the other hand, maybe there was a Catholic procession in Bristol. I don't know the answer, and neither does anybody else. It was just another tug on that choke chain, and didn't do me any harm at all.

My television shows at ATV were entering their fifth year and, in my estimation, needed an injection of fresh ideas. Strangely enough, it was a time when the shows, which were being aired at 7.30 pm each Tuesday, reached their highest ratings ever, having, for one week at least, reached the No. 1 spot for the first time.

Then one day in London, I bumped into Terry

Hughes, one of the BBC producers I'd worked with previously, and now Assistant Head of Light Entertainment at the Television Centre. To my astonishment, he gave me the impression that I would be welcome back at the BBC, providing we got the right shows together. The reason for my surprise at the prospect of returning was that, as I had left there in 1970, after so many happy years, the BBC may have felt that they'd had my 'best' years. Terry rang Eve within a week or so, saying that Bill Cotton, then Head of Light Entertainment (and now Managing Director of BBC Television), would like to see me. An appointment was arranged, and after a long sojourn 'on the other side', I entered the BBC Television Centre again.

Bill, Terry and I sat in the office for an hour or so, chatting about the prospects of doing more shows, and reminiscing about the early days, and my first shows there.

'I think we should try a series in the New Year,' Bill said, 'and with a bit of luck, I think we might get five more years out of it.' Well, we did, and many more.

Just as I was about to leave the office, Bill said, 'Maybe you should do one special, in the meantime, just to get the feel of the place again.' He then suggested that Yvonne Littlewood might be the person to produce and direct the shows – another wise decision. 'One last thing before you go, and this is the sixty-four thousand dollar question . . .'

'Go on,' I said.

'How would you feel about doing them live on Saturday nights, like you use to in the old days?' I accepted gladly, we shook hands, and I left.

I've always loved doing live television. Many of my fellow artists could never understand why. 'Why put that pressure on yourself?' they'd say. 'Nobody notices whether it's live or not, so why bother?' Well,

159

the explanation has always been an elusive one but – it just feels different. There's an urgency and excitement about knowing that this is your one and only chance to get it right. Maybe it's different for me, having done so many live series in the past, and having become accustomed to the stimulation. It could be, in fact, that artists who entered the television world during the pre-taping years, have never known what live TV feels like, whereas I know what they're missing from where I stand. I'm sure it's very much a personal thing anyway.

My return to Saturday nights live on BBC was just the injection needed for me at the time, and it breathed new life into my career. Yvonne Littlewood, a very talented and conscientious lady, with a formidable record as far as musical TV shows are concerned, was at the helm throughout. So far, we have done nine series of shows, plus a considerable number of specials. We both endeavoured at all times to present a format which covered a broad spectrum of varied music, from pop and country, through to jazz and big band nostalgic sounds, and classical. It was quite common to discover as my guests on Saturday nights such contrasting talents as country singer Charlie Pride, jazz virtuoso of the harmonica and guitar Toots Theilemans, and flautist James Galway. In fact, when looking back through my old scripts for research, I'm very proud indeed that in this day and age when survival can depend so much on blatant commercialism, we managed to maintain our integrity for so long. It has also stretched me vocally, encouraging me to tackle duets, both vocal and instrumental, with a wide range of artists. Imagine my pleasure on hearing the news of Yvonne's inclusion in the 1986 Honours List. Her receiving an MBE for her contribution to television is something she richly deserves.

One year when I was due to do a summer season in Eastbourne, the family had a discussion, and it was decided that I would 'go it alone', with Lynn and the girls dividng the summer months between home and my apartment down there. I found a very comfortable flat, conveniently situated halfway between the theatre and Eastbourne Golf Club. Most of my leisure time was to be spent treading the fairways with fellow golf addicts from the various shows in town. When the weather wasn't suitable for outdoor activities, I'd get out my scribbling pad and contribute a few more reminiscences to what had by now become a considerable volume. Dear Peggy worked laboriously through my manuscript, which dropped through her letter box at regular intervals, correcting mistakes in spelling, grammar and above all punctuation. She would type the whole thing out clearly, returning it to me for insertion in its special folder.

'Do you realise how much you've written so far?' she asked me over the phone one morning. I'd frankly never thought of counting words at that stage.

'No idea,' I told her. 'Have you been keeping count?'

She then proceeded to astonish me with the details. 'Up to now, you've done about sixty thousand words,' Peggy said, 'and I must say, it's so easy to read and most importantly, sounds like you.'

At the end of my Eastbourne season I more or less decided to call it a day as far as those long running engagements were concerned. I'd been accepting summer seasons virtually non-stop since 1965 and thought I'd had enough. Not that I didn't enjoy them; on the contrary, in spite of that nightly grind of two shows, it was great fun.

By now, Eve Taylor was showing signs of having had enough of the business. She'd been a hardworking agent and manager for as long as I could remember and her track record was very impressive indeed. Eve always was a highly strung, excitable lady, and I was not at all surprised when the stresses and strains of the entertainment world began to take their toll. Her friends and associates noticed the change in her long before she became aware of it herself.

Finally it happened. Returning from a short holiday in America, she rang me up, asking me to drop into the office later in the week.

'I don't think I can take the strain of this business any longer, love,' she told me as I sat across from her in the office. It was easy to see that apart from anything else, she was, in fact, losing interest in the whole thing. 'I really can't be bothered with the hassle and the rat race [her favourite description of the world of theatrical management].' In spite of my knowing that I was about to lose my manager of twenty years' standing, I couldn't but agree with her that this was her only suitable action. It was time to retire.

We were both of one mind as to her successor, a mutual friend named Bernard Lee. Bernie had long experience since starting out as an office boy in the Grade Organisation many years ago. He'd worked very closely with the late Brian Epstein in the heyday of the Beatles. He'd then gone on to handle many of the major stars, while working as a partner in the famous London Management company. However, most important of all, he was a friend. He knew me and what was important to me both professionally and personally. My business affairs were transferred to Bernie lock, stock and barrel and as far as I know, dear Evie breathed a sigh of relief.

Bernie was in complete agreement with my decision not to take on any further summer season shows. He also confirmed my reservations about doing any more club work, not that there was all that much available by this time. The club circuit which had enjoyed such an enormous boom through the sixties and sventies was beginning to show signs of coming to an end. People were not coming in anything like the same numbers, which meant smaller profits, or, indeed, no profits at all. As the old Music Hall some twenty years earlier had changed over to bingo halls, so the clubs became discos, or simply drinking houses.

As often happens, one trend replaced another, and so a new field catering for the public's needs slowly emerged. Civic centres were appearing in more and more towns and cities, attracting an increasing number of established artists to appear for one or two nights. Much of the 'family' type audiences, starved of theatre life and not attracted to the clubs, began to re-appear. Many of the towns, in fact, were now inspired to re-open their old theatres, re-furbished to look alive, well and above all welcoming. For somebody such as myself who had worked at these places before their demise, it was a real thrill to return. The Opera House in Belfast (where I'd last appeared in 1955), the Darlington Theatre, the Grand Theatre Swansea and many more, together with the new breed of entertainment centres, meant a whole circuit of very attractive venues.

The pressure of twelve shows a week during the summer was replaced by two or three nights a week, giving both the entertainers and the theatres a pretty good chance of success. It's good to note, of course, that most of the major summer resorts continue to present long-running shows, while the less successful ones, no longer able to support a resident company in the summer months, take advantage of those artists available for just one or two nights. As I've said, the theatre has always been notable for its survival, moving with the times and in my experience, invariably for the better of all concerned. It's easy indeed for people to say, 'Oh it's not like it was in the old days, they shouldn't have changed this or that', but those changes have so often been part and parcel of the theatre's survival, and a result of things no longer working 'as they used to be'.

Having been fortunate enough throughout my long career to have worked through the various phases of the 'Big Band' era, the Music Hall, the 'Club' or cabaret period, and of course, the television phenomenon, I can honestly say that the one-night concert pattern now in vogue for such as myself is undoubtedly the most enjoyable I can recall. People accustomed to seeing some of their favourite artists on television can go along and see them in what I certainly feel to be the most advantageous light.

Even after I'd started working with Bernie, there were still some engagements in my diary for which Eve was responsible, so we continued to keep in close contact until these were fulfilled. Just about the last of them, in fact, was a *Michael Parkinson Show* on BBC television.

My appearance, however, was put very much in doubt due to a severe back condition sustained a few weeks beforehand. I've suffered from recurring back problems for many years now, but this particular bout was undoubtedly the worst to date. Fortunately, after weeks of regular treatment, I was given the go-ahead from my doctor, a decision which was to prove most important to my career over the following year.

My fellow guests on that occasion were that irresistible broadcaster and writer Arthur Marshall, and jazz singer Annie Ross. As is the practice with these shows, I had discussed my guest appearance with Michael's researchers so that a rough outline of our proposed chat could be pre-arranged. However, things were not to go just as planned.

Arthur Marshall discussed a new book he'd just written; Annie Ross, having related some very interesting anecdotes from her career, closed her interview saying that perhaps one day she would write them in a book. It was then my turn to appear. In order that the continuity was maintained, Michael's opening remark was, 'Have you ever thought of writing a book, Val?'

Within moments, the intended line of questions was abandoned, and I found myself relating stories from my childhood and of my special relationship with my father. I had, until that time, avoided the temptation to tell these stories on a major TV show, because of the risk firstly, of sounding over-sentimental, and secondly, of cheapening to some extent the quite genuine affection I felt for my parents.

The reaction to that interview was such that within a week, enquiries had come from several of the major publishing companies asking if they could have a look at the manuscript which was mentioned on the show.

We made it quite clear to them that I professed to know nothing whatever about the art of journalism and had written the whole thing in the simplest of styles. One of the interested parties was a company called Elm Tree Books (the parent of which is Hamish Hamilton, publishers of the very successful David Niven books). My agent sent copies of the manuscript to each of the companies who had shown enthusiasm and we waited for their reaction.

I simply couldn't believe it when my office was informed that Elm Tree Books thought the manuscript could be published more or less 'as it was'. 'It could do with a bit of trimming here, a little extra there and so on, otherwise it's fine,' they said, then repeating what both Peggy and Lynn had already told me, they concluded, 'The important thing is that it reads well, and sounds exactly as you do yourself.' That was to be something I'd hear over and over again as the project progressed. I could not believe my luck, really. Had I set out to have an autobiography published in the normal way, I'd have found it very disconcerting, having those stories of my childhood written by a ghost-writer. Somehow that wouldn't have appealed to me, but now the problem had, in fact, been laid aside by the publishers themselves.

Pretty soon, the book was in full swing, photographs for the cover were being chosen, and a further selection of photos from my private collection were being sieved through. It was all so new to me, and so very exciting. When it came to picking the title, everything seemed to fall into place. I'd always looked upon my early years, both those of my childhood and those constituting the early part of my career, as the very special ones in my life, for numerous reasons. One has to read the manuscript in question to clarify this. By coincidence, one of my most successful hit records was called *The Special Years*. It was agreed that we need look no further for the title.

One more surprise, however, was awaiting me. The publishers rang one day, enquiring about the possibility of my family having photographs of one or two things relating to the story. One was a shed in our little garden that played a very important part in my young life. The second, a photograph of the street where I was born, which had long since had a considerable face lift.

'No, I'm sorry,' I had to tell them, 'my Dad's little shed disappeared while I was still a boy', and then trying to help I said, 'Tell you what, I can do a sketch of it, and of the street as it was in the period in question.' They told me to do the sketches anyway.

(I've been interested in drawing throughout my life and had no trouble making a pretty good representation of the missing subjects.) A couple of days later I had a call from Elm Tree.

'Those drawings are good, we'd like to use them. Why not do some more and we'll have illustrations throughout the book.' This I did with great relish and the evidence is there forever.

Since that time, in fact, Lynn has persuaded me to have my very first art lessons. I had little alternative really, when as a Christmas present I was given a course of lessons at Amersham Art College in Buckinghamshire. The head of the college, Romeo de Girolamo by name and a very fine artist himself, has given me great encouragement.

Being a country boy at heart I've always had a love and appreciation of trees, sketching them at every opportunity. While holidaying in the West Indies recently I tried my hand at some of the tropical ones. We thought with one or two other sketches they'd act as a kind of interior decor for the book.

As quickly as I could acquire a few advance copies of *The Special Years*, I posted them off to my immediate family in the hope that at this late stage they'd approve my story, or more to the point my version of the family's story. I'd long since learned that when you become a well-known personality, and agree to expose some of the more intimate details of your personal life, you also open the windows on the privacy of your family. To what extent you have the right to do so is perhaps best discussed with them beforehand.

Happily, they all passed my book as being fit for public consumption, much to my relief. I'm the youngest of eight children, by the way, four boys and four girls. Sadly only three sisters and one brother remain, three still living at home in Waterford, the other in the United States.

My mother, then in her nineties, had been for some years living at a charming nursing home on the outskirts of Waterford. My sister Una decided that since Mom's eyesight wasn't too good, she'd pop along each morning and read aloud to her a chapter or so of the story. Her task completed she closed the book.

'Well, Mother, that's it. What did you think?' she asked.

'Isn't he marvellous to remember all those details now,' Mom thought. 'He's a credit to us.' She leaned back against her pillows, and closing her eyes said in a very calm voice, 'How much do you think he'll get for that now, Una?'

'Oh, I haven't a clue,' my sister told her, then turning to the flap on the outer sleeve added, 'Well, it's £5.95 a copy.'

Mother's eyes quickly popped open again. 'How much?'

Una repeated the price. Mother looked flabbergasted. 'Ah for God's sake, he'll never sell that, it's far too expensive.' She paused, and closing her eyes once more, said in a whisper, 'I would have thought ten shillings would be about right.'

Mother is no longer with us, unfortunately, so she won't get to hear the contents of this second volume. Maybe it's just as well, she might assess it at five shillings this time.

There are many viewpoints from which I can reflect on the undoubted success of *The Special Years*. To begin with, nobody can ever take away the fact that I wrote a best seller at my first attempt. I can treasure this for the rest of my life.

I embarked on the enterprise with all kinds of disadvantages. I'd never done anything like it before, and I had no literary experience whatever, apart from the odd page of script contributed to my radio or television shows and the occasional letter to my family. Yet, here I was, ballpoint pen in hand, facing a large, virgin writing pad. As the words of the song say, 'Where do I begin?'

I knew there was a good story to be told, the memories vivid enough in my mind, the anecdotes relatively fresh due to the countless interviews I had had over the years. The question was, could I manage to keep them alive on paper? Of course there were writers galore out there possessing all the skills and experience I sadly lacked and willing to do the whole thing for me. Somehow, had that been my only choice, I do believe I would have forgotten the whole thing. Deep inside I felt my story was so personal to me that we couldn't be separated without some kind of loss or damage. Maybe it was ego, or perhaps a kind of insecurity that told me to disclose the story on my own terms; who knows? Anyway, I was determined to tackle the thing and simply take my time. I knew I possessed two important assets – lots of patience and a very large waste paper basket.

On the other hand, of course, I had many advantages seldom afforded to the inexperienced writer. For a start, I was a well known entertainer who had fortunately reached the position where the public to a large extent accepted what I did; there was no apparent reason why a certain percentage of them would not want to read my story.

It was unlikely they would assess it for its literary value, but with luck they might be entertained and amused by what I had to say.

When you think of the endless stream of manuscripts arriving at publishing houses daily, some extremely well written, others telling a cracking good story, only to be returned with regrets to the senders, the many and varied reasons for their rejection all add up to one simple commercial truth: not enough people would buy the book. Publishers do of course gamble on some of them, and as the saying goes, 'you win some, you lose some'. I suppose with people like myself there is an obvious improvement in the odds or the starting price as far as the gamble goes. Compare the chances of two contrasting books, one by a well known personality, the other by an unknown, though possibly a far superior writer. In many ways it's like looking at two shop windows in the high street, one brightly lit and advertising its goods, the other with its blinds drawn and a sign inviting you to come inside if you wish to discover what's for sale. Discerning buyers will probably go inside and check the quality, but most people won't bother. I'm not for a moment suggesting that this always reflects the value of the respective books – it simply indicates the advantages I had at the outset.

I decided to sit down and write the whole thing in long hand, as if relating a story to friends. With the patient help of my dear assistant Peggy and the experts from my publishing company, we corrected all my spelling and punctuation errors, and in time brought the thing to fruition.

Through the early eighties, my annual TV series contained a weekly filmed segment, mainly located in Great Britain and Ireland. These filmed inserts enabled us to introduce a bit of outdoors into an otherwise live studio presentation. They also gave us the extra challenge of finding weekly settings for a specially selected song. During the weeks, we tried sailing, travelling the canals by barge, horseriding, gliding, cycling, visiting country gardens, taking my audience on a visit to my home town, and on one occasion, dashing about above the Norfolk countryside in a twin-seater autogyro, a tiny flying machine with no outer body, looking for all the world like a three-wheeled tandem with no handlebars.

Some months previously I had happened to see a BBC documentary film about the autogyro and its creator, Wing Commander Ken Wallis, and found it quite fascinating. I only had to mention this to Yvonne, of course, for the wheels to be set in motion. The video of the show was delivered to her office where we could watch it at our leisure. A few days later, everything was arranged with the Wing Commander, who was most enthusiastic about our idea.

Our proposed film sequence was planned over two days, on location up in Norfolk near the Wing Commander's home. The opening segment of my song took place in a nearby hangar, where I viewed some wonderful vintage aircraft, my lyrics inviting the viewers to take to the air. Then, strolling outside, I discovered the tiny autogyro and climbed aboard.

It was a very chilly afternoon and I think the entire crew were somewhat relieved as we prepared to finish for the day. The actual flying sequence was scheduled for nine o'clock the following morning.

'Do you think you'll feel scared tomorrow?' Ken Wallis asked as I dismounted from the flimsy machine. Even though I'd done some flying in various light aircraft and gliders, I felt this was something quite different.

'I honestly don't know what to expect,' I told him. 'We'll just have to wait and see, won't we?' I was beginning to remove my headgear when Ken reached out a hand and stopped me.

'Tell you what,' he said, smiling wickedly, 'why don't we have a little trial run right now? You're all dressed up, the machine is ready – so what do you say?'

Before I had time to answer, Yvonne jumped into

action. 'Just give us time to set up,' she requested. 'We might get some good stuff in the can. Who knows, it could be chucking it down tomorrow morning.'

Later, as we sat warming up for take off, Ken turned and shouted through the roar of the engine. 'Tell you what, I'll go up about fifty feet, and hover a bit. If you feel that it's too scary, just give me a sign and I'll come straight down again, OK?' I laughed out loud, thinking to myself, 'Yeah, suppose I do chicken out, what happens tomorrow? We can't just pack up and go home empty-handed. I've got to like or lump it.'

At last we took off, in a cloud of dust, rising almost vertically to fifty feet or so. In fact, it was very exciting, if extremely cold. Leaning forward, I gave Ken a very professional-looking thumbs-up sign. I gasped for breath as we climbed to two hundred feet or so, then came diving down to zoom past the waiting camera. Tears streamed from my eyes as the cold wind bit into my face. It was such a strange sensation to gaze down at the airfield below, with nothing to break my view but the sight of my shoe on the footrest.

Yvonne and our cameraman were delighted with this unexpected bonus, so it was a satisfied company which made its way to the hotel for hot baths and dinner. I slept soundly that night, happy with the prospect of more flying in the morning. Our location next day was, in fact, at the Wing Commander's home, where he has a short, grass-covered take-off strip. We also had the added pleasure of visiting his mini-hangar, housing some thirteen autogyros, including those used in the famous James Bond movie *You Only Live Twice* for which he did all the flying. We nicknamed it his Gyrobank.

On the actual night of the show, Ken agreed to

come along to the studio, complete with his flying machine. It gave our audience and viewers at home to the opportunity of seeing exactly what it looked like.

As anybody involved in outdoor filming in Britain will confirm, the unpredictability of our climate can make life very difficult, and much of the time downright impossible.

With that problem in mind, it was suggested that we could do some filming immediately following my 1984 tour in Australia. It seemed a good idea for a number of reasons: I was already there, the weather was pretty certain to be warm and sunny most of the time, and the whole area was photographically untapped, as far as my show was concerned. We looked forward to a fruitful venture. As the concert tour came to an end, my television producer, Yvonne Littlewood, arrived to organise things. My locations were selected in many contrasting areas – sailing on Sydney Harbour; sightseeing in the Blue Mountains; visiting a reconstructed old mining village called Sovereign Hill, near Melbourne, and a tropical island off the Great Barrier Reef; making a trip into the outback to Alice Springs and Ayres Rock; and much more. The musical tracks for my songs had, of course, been put on to tape while I was still in London prior to my tour. These were relayed to me on location, while I simply mimed to the lyrics. Quite a fuss was created over my visit to Ayres Rock, which, as you may know, is a sacred site to the Aboriginal people. Our application to film there was, in fact, handled by the Australian Tourist Authorities in London, but sadly, permission was refused at the last moment. We accepted the decision, naturally enough, but the Northern Territories Tourist Board thought it unfair and interceded. When the newspapers got hold of the story it became quite a national incident. Headlines in the major newspapers announced: VAL BARRED FROM THE ROCK –

IRISH SINGER BANNED – NO ROCKERS AT THE ROCK. Smaller headlines were to be found in the papers as far afield as London and New York. I should mention that we had no intention of going on to the Rock. This, we knew, would be out of the question. We simply wanted to film the unique landmark in three different lighting conditions, dawn, afternoon and sunset, the lyrics of my song relating these to stages of our lives.

Anyway, we were finally invited to go there and everybody gave us a great welcome, including the Aboriginal guides who were there to oversee our efforts.

While the storm was raging in the newspapers I was constantly being called by the media and, of course, being stopped by people in the street.

One evening, while doing some night filming in the heart of Kings Cross in Sydney, I was intercepted once again. I was actually being filmed, singing the verse to a song, indicating my disillusionment with city life and my longing for the open spaces. The idea, in fact, was to mix the film through to my tropical paradise on the Great Barrier Reef. Since the location was a busy street corner, and the time was rush hour, the sound of orchestra and voice were being transmitted to me with the aid of a tiny mike, similar to a hearing aid, which was neatly placed in my ear. In other words, nobody would ever detect that I was, in fact, singing my heart out. The camera had been strategically placed across the street. Suddenly, as I poured reached the climax of the song, a complete stranger walked up to me with his hand outstretched.

'Good God, look who we have here,' he said smiling, and obviously glad to see me. He was now standing directly between me and the camera, completely unaware of his intrusion. 'My wife and I are great fans of your TV shows.' His voice was barely audible through the noise of the traffic and the thirty piece orchestra blasting into my ear, not to mention my own voice.

'Thank you,' I said, shaking his hand, then, pointing to the camera perched on its tripod across the way, I told him, 'Sorry, I'm filming at the moment, as you can see, so could you stand aside for a few minutes.'

Like so many people on these occasions, he looked at the camera, smiled his acknowledgment of the situation, apologised, then continued to talk.

'You know, we wouldn't miss one of your shows – and what about all this Ayres Rock business, eh?'

By now, one of the crew was urging him to let me get on with things, but he was in full flow.

'My wife and I watch the papers every day, we haven't missed a word about it. I see you're going there after all.'

'Yes, thank you,' I said once again, this time gently pushing him out of shot. 'Say hello to your wife for me.'

That was all the encouragement he needed. 'You can say hello yourself,' he told me, grabbing my arm. Then moving his free arm in the direction of an adjacent shop door he yelled out, 'Hey Mavis, Mavis, come over here a minute! You'll never believe who's here, it's what's his name on the telly – you know . . . Andy Williams.'

A few minutes later, I was back to work, my hearing aid in place, trying not to look at any of the gang, who were still laughing. The filming turned out very well and made a welcome change in the make-up of the show.

My early visits down under were, as in the case of many visiting artists, limited to the main centres – Perth, Adelaide, Melbourne, Sydney and Brisbane, any extra engagements consisting of cabaret appearances in the clubs of New South Wales. Since, as I mentioned, I felt much more at home in theatres and concert halls, my promoters began to consider, as an alternative to the clubs, the many civic theatres and concert centres in towns within easy reach of the main cities. It opened up quite an extensive tour, which from the work-satisfaction point of view is right up my street. There's always been a fear among some artists that if you play anywhere other than the large, more prestigious centres, people might think you were slipping, or losing your grip, or that you were over the hill. Frankly, I've never been able to see this argument. People are people, towns are towns, and as long as the theatre is nice and has the facilities, I can't see anything wrong with it. Maybe that comes from the fact that I was born and brought up in a small city of some 30,000 people, and I loved it when visiting artists included our town on their itinerary. The family have joined me for some of the trips and share my enthusiasm for the place. At the time of writing I'm planning another tour for next year, and I hope there will be many more.

Sketch of an Irish cottage I did many years ago

—— Epilogue ——

Compiling this second book has once again meant countless visits to the attic where the Doonicans store the accumulated evidence of their family's history. An accepted part of theatrical life has always been being photographed constantly, so the combined collection of snaps resulting from the careers of both Lynn and myself makes 'looking through the family albums' a pretty lengthy operation.

Watching the girls grow up 'before our very eyes', as Arthur Askey would have said, is something we still enjoy. There are photos of Fiona as a baby – Sarah aged two in her bubble bath – their first Holy Communion – on the beach at Barbados – eighteenth birthday parties – and so it goes. (A few examples are included here to illustrate the passing years.)

Sarah, now twenty-one, is completing her studies for a BA Honours in Film and Drama, subjects which have fascinated her for many years. Her knowledge of movies and the making of them has been developing since she was about twelve. Both Lynn and I hope that her future career will merely be an extension of her beloved hobby.

Fiona, on the other hand, who is twenty, completed her studies at secretarial college well over a year ago, since when she's done a six month stint at the BBC and a similar period enjoying a working holiday in Australia. She's seen all four corners of that fascinating country, something I'm sure she'll always remember with affection.

Since returning home she's spent quite a deal of her time typing every word of *Walking Tall* from my endless scribbles, pausing occasionally to comment, 'Dad, you really must do something about your spelling!'

They have both brought great joy into our lives, and we look forward to many happy years of their companionship.

It's gratifying these days to reflect on the past ten years, and find them among the most enjoyable and fulfilling of my career. The reasons are many, but three in particular come to mind.

Firstly, I'd arrived at the happy stage where I could do what I wanted professionally, and when I chose to do it.

Concert tours both at home and abroad afforded me the opportunity to mature as a solo performer in a way I hadn't done before in a cabaret or summer season environment.

And finally, my television shows certainly brought greater artistic satisfaction than ever before, because of their musical content.

The number of working hours crammed into the making of my 'live' Saturday night shows would, I'm sure, amaze the casual viewer. Planning the whole thing, choosing and learning duets with guest artists, not to mention the memorising of seven or eight songs a week, plus the script, took all the hours available. Yvonne Littlewood, Roger and myself tucked ourselves away in a small basement room in the bowels of the BBC Television Centre week after week for about three months a year, often not finding time for a lunch break, simply to get the thing ready for Saturday nights.

In 1982 I was to meet a musical 'soul mate' who for two seasons at least shared his vast musical knowledge and experience with our resident group. I'm speaking, or writing, of Ray Charles. (As he himself would immediately add, 'No, not that one, I'm the other one!') Ray has spent some thirty-five years of his life attending to the musical requirement of Mr Perry Como, the Ray Charles Singers becoming in the process, one of the most famous of choral ensembles since the late forties. He was already known to Yvonne, who had previously produced and directed some of Perry Como's work. Ray was visiting Britain as musical advisor to the Muppet Shows, then in production at ATV Studios at Elstree, when I first met him. Yvonne, Roger and I had by this time completed some six series of music shows, so a fresh team member warming up on the touchline was precisely what was needed. For two series, Ray turned our trio into an enthusiastic quartet, and very enjoyable it was too. He kindly described our hardworking group as 'the tightest ship' he'd ever encountered in his long career.

A question often put to me these days, both by the show business publicity machine and the general public, is 'Why do you think your popularity or success has lasted so long?' I find it virtually impossible to find any kind of intelligent answer; after all it's not for me to analyse why people have enjoyed my work all these years. I just know that they have, and I'm deeply grateful for it and thank the public sincerely for rewarding me so handsomely with their goodwill.

I think it was Perry Como who, in answer to that same question, replied, 'The secret of my many years of success is three-inch lapels.' When asked to elaborate, he went on, 'Well, when I first began to enjoy popularity, three-inch lapels were the fashion, so I decided to have some. They suited me down to the ground, so when suddenly everybody changed to four-inch lapels, then two-inch lapels, and even no lapels at all, I decided to stick with what I'd got, and still have them today.'

Need I tell you that the moral of this little story is, 'When you find out what it is you do best, and what the public wants from you, then stick with it, and do it as well as you can.' Of course, you must send it for a regular service, keep it looking as good as possible, and most important of all, think very hard before trading it in for a new model.

Personally I can't think of a better answer than that, when endeavouring to explain my years as an entertainer. I've been a small fish in the great big ocean of show business, but thank goodness the waters have remained reasonably calm for me and I've enjoyed every minute of it. There's no denying the fact that many of my colleagues would find the prospect of wearing three-inch lapels year in, year out very boring indeed. Well, that's very much a personal thing, depending on your make up or personality. Some of my pals swap and change their golf clubs every time a new model comes on the market. In my experience, once the novelty wears off, your golf is much the same as before. It's the way we swing the club that causes all our problems.

Well, it's now forty years since I earned my first 'salary' as a singer. My old school friend Mickey and I took part in a local concert in our home town of Waterford way back in 1946 and were paid the princely sum of ten shillings for our efforts.

Just recently, Mickey drew my attention to our chosen repertoire on that distant occasion.

'Have you ever thought about what we actually sang that night?' he asked me.

'No idea,' I admitted. 'After all, it was quite a while ago.'

'Well,' he said laughing, 'we must have looked a right couple of eegits up there – believe it or not we had the cheek to stand side by side singing *We're Three Caballeros*. If that's not Irish, what is?'

Little did I know, as we nervously stood there on the tiny stage of that church hall, too excited to notice we were, in fact, only two caballeros, what a marvellous and rewarding life lay ahead for me in the world of entertainment: the ups and downs of this fascinating profession, the unexpected joys of sharing the stage, the microphone or the television camera with two generations of such stalwarts as Bing Crosby, Perry Como, John Denver, Burl Ives, Tony Bennett, Harry Secombe, Ted Ray, Kenny Rogers, Olivia Newton John, Howard Keel and hundreds more. Like most youngsters, I spent many of those early days gazing admiringly at such people from a wooden seat in the gods. Unlike the vast majority of others however, I was given the good fortune of going on eventually to join their world on the other side of the screen or footlights. I should add that the passing years have in no way diminished or dulled the pleasure and appreciation I feel when sharing a duet with such talented people as Stephane Grappelli, James Galway or Rosemary Clooney.

Nowadays, as I prepare to enter my sixties and still enjoy great success, I've begun to realise that the old choke chain has ceased to function.

Now that I've spent some forty years of my life in the entertainment world, reaching a kind of pastureland where many of the early pressures brought on by constantly having to prove oneself, have subsided, I'm fast realising that there are many other joys available to my family and myself. Who knows, maybe I'll find a whole new meaning to the old adage 'life begins at forty'.